Your Life Matters

The Tool Kit for Changing Your World

Dr. Cliff Robertson, Jr.

Dr. Cliff Robertson, Jr.

Cover designed by Judith San Nicolas atJudithSDesign.com

A portion of the sale of this book goes to support homeless and disabled veterans.

Dr. Cliff Robertson, Jr.
Visit my website at drcliffrobertsonjr.com

Kerysso Press.blogspot.com

RELIGION / Christian Ministry / Counseling & Recovery
SELF-HELP / Motivational & Inspirational

BISAC REL050000
BISAC SEL021000
ISBN-978-1-7361603-8-1

Kerysso Press

Dedication

To Karen,

I do not have words to adequately express my love and appreciation for you. You help me be a better man. You challenge my thinking and help me to see things clearer. You bring beauty to everything you touch.

This book has been inspired by many things, but mainly by God and you. The stories you have shared with me about your time as a teacher inspire me. You changed lives and created a legacy that will impact generations. I feel like I could write another edition of this book with just those stories. Maybe we will.

But for now, I want you to know that I dedicate this book to you, Karen Robertson, my beautiful wife, whom I love and adore. You are the inspiration for this book and the one who gave me the ideas and the push to begin.

Cliff

Dr. Cliff Robertson, Jr.

Preface

We are in a fight for our lives.

As this book was being edited, the news announced the death of a thirty-year-old young woman, Cheslie Kryst. At the time of this writing, her death is being investigated as a suicide. She fell from the 60th-floor roof of her apartment building in New York City. Chelsie was an attorney, a reporter, an NCAA Div 1 Athlete, and a former Miss USA. Near her birthday, she wrote an essay questioning whether her life mattered. "Turning thirty feels like a cold reminder that I'm running out of time to matter in society's eyes—and it's infuriating."

On October 1, 2021, Senior Chief Troy Norrell, a decorated Navy Special Forces sailor who served with distinction in Iraq and Afghanistan (five tours), took his own life. He had retired early from the Navy due to C-PTSD and Traumatic Brain Injury. He had sought help but nothing seemed to work and he spiraled downward.

Troy had played professional baseball. Everyone who knew him loved him. He often defended the underdog and the outcast.

He was a hero to many before he ever went to war. His service to this country made him a national hero in my book.

One guy who knew him wrote, "the demons that tormented him made him take his own life."

The loss of our veterans, due to the invisible scars of war, is an epidemic.

Suicide is an epidemic!

There have been times in my own life when I thought the world would be a better place without me. I have battled with depression and anxiety that I couldn't seem to shake for days and weeks at a time.

I could share stories here without end.

If you are honest, you've probably had some of these same thoughts.

I want you to know that you are not alone. I want you to know #YourLifeMatters

You have more to offer this world than you know. Your presence on this planet is essential, meaningful, significant, and you are loved.

We are in a fight for our lives. Let's win this fight. As you read this book, I hope you will find a story or two that will resonate in your soul and encourage you to not just survive, but thrive—having the best life. God loves you and #YOURLIFEMATTERS

Cliff

Introduction

Hi, my name is Cliff Robertson, Jr. I have several titles, from Dr. Cliff, Executive Director, Pastor, Husband, Father, Grandfather, and some that are not so pleasant.

But the truth is, none of them seem to matter when I am hit with tragedy or depression. I've struggled with my life in more ways than you can imagine. Even though my name is on the cover of this book and I have several different positive titles, there are times when I have just wanted to quit—on my work and my life.

There have been times when I have even made plans to end my life, but something always stopped me.

Sometimes I have battled with depression and anxiety. I felt my worth amounted to "zero." I couldn't get out of bed or off the couch. It was like an 800-pound gorilla took up residence on my chest. I didn't know what to do.

Many times, someone would call needing my help. Or I'd force myself to go out of the house and before I knew it, I'd be busy and forget about the gorilla, at least for the moment.

Other times people would "divinely intervene" and get me going again. Even today while writing this book, I doubted if this message, this book, was enough and questioned whether I missed something even more important.

Recently, I stopped to take a counseling call with a young man battling depression. He could see no purpose left in his life.

When I helped him lift that veil of depression long enough to see how many lives he impacted for good, he tearfully explained that he felt like he could see beyond his circumstance and dream again. It changed his life. I'll share more about his desperation and the tools we used to overcome it in the book.

If you are honest, you have probably had similar questions and doubts. Maybe you've felt like there's no point, it's all over, and you've planned your exit from this world. I don't know.

But I do know this, you are reading this book at this moment, for a purpose. I am grateful that you are taking this moment to consider that there might be more to life than what you have considered. So hear me when I say… Your life is not over.

Your life has a purpose and a mission. I am here to tell you

This book was written for you.

I don't care if anyone else reads it but you.

If this book makes a difference in your life, then all the work has been worth it. On the pages that follow, you will read numerous stories of how individuals—regardless of their circumstances and the odds against them—have changed their world and in turn made the world a better place for us all.

I believe that you can do this as well.

Are you ready?

I think you are.

#YourLifeMatters!

Contents

11   Section One – Real Life Troubles and Triumphs

13   Chapter 1 What Can One Person Really Do?

23   Chapter 2 Depression/Mental Health

27   Chapter 3 Your Life Matters, Even When You Have
        Made Bad Choices

39   Chapter 4 Disability & Its Many Forms

51   Chapter 5 Socio-Economic Status

59   Chapter 6 Loss/Grief/Tragedy

77   Chapter 7 PTSD

91   Chapter 8 Suicide

105, 215   *Suicide Lifeline 24/7 Phone Number

107   Section Two The Tool Kit

109   Chapter 9 The Power of God in Your Life

119   Chapter 10 The Psychology of it All

129   Chapter 11 Self Esteem, Self-worth, and Social Media

147   Chapter 12 Fostering a Positive Self Image

163   Chapter 13 Your Life Has a Purpose. Discover it Now.

201   Chapter 14 Let's Change Our World

207   Epilogue

209   Bibliography and Resources

217   About the Author

218   Other Books by Dr. Robertson

Dr. Cliff Robertson, Jr.

Section One

Real-life Troubles and Triumphs

Dr. Cliff Robertson, Jr.

Chapter 1
What Can One Person Really Do?

My granny raised my sister and me after our parents divorced. Looking back, I am truly amazed at what she did for us.

Granny took us everywhere, never complaining or griping about it. She simply told us to get in the car with all of our stuff and "let's go." I played little league Red Devil football. We practiced three times a week and then played a game once a week in Houston, an hour away.

One time, my game started early in the evening. Granny dropped me off, and she and my sister went to get something to eat. On their way back, she turned into the parking lot, but missed the entrance and drove into a ditch. A deep ditch. Too deep to drive out of. They had to call a wrecker to pull them out.

They didn't discuss the mishap in front of me. If my sister hadn't told me about it, I would never have known it happened.

Granny told me, "Well, Bubba, these things happen. We weren't hurt. The car wasn't damaged. No big deal." She let these things roll off her back like water off the back of a duck.

~

I learned a lot from Granny's tales. She told me a story she heard while she was in nurse training. It was about a nurse and a little girl.

The little girl, Annie, had been diagnosed as hopelessly insane. They locked her up in the dungeon of a mental institution on the outskirts of Boston, Massachusetts. People said that this young girl was so far gone that there were times when she acted like a wild animal. She would attack anyone who dared to come close to her. They labeled her Crazy Annie.

Other times, Annie would be completely catatonic and wouldn't recognize anything. She sat, staring at the walls for days on end. No one knew of a treatment plan or had any hope that Crazy Annie would ever get better. They had locked her up and thrown away the key.

But an elderly nurse, a woman of faith, believed God could do what modern medicine could not. She believed and had hope for all of God's children and Little Annie was one of them.

So, she started with taking the long trek down to the dungeon every day to eat her lunch outside of Little Annie's cage. The nurse had a deep desire to communicate her love for Annie as well as God's love for the girl, but she didn't know how to reach her. She only knew she had to go.

Each day, she ate her lunch beside Annie's cage and talked to Annie with no response. Some days she sang for her, but Annie didn't respond to that either. One day, the nurse left her dessert, a chocolate brownie, beside Annie's cage.

Annie didn't acknowledge the brownie beside her while the nurse remained, but when the nurse came back the next day, the brownie was gone. Every Thursday, the nurse would bring her dessert and leave it for Annie. When she returned the next day, it would be gone.

Something began to change through these simple acts of love and kindness that no one could explain. After several weeks passed, doctors noticed small improvements in Annie. Then, after a few months, the improvements were so profound, they transferred her out of the cage and moved her upstairs into a lower level of security. Eventually, the staff allowed her to be among the general population.

Finally, one day the doctors told the formerly hopelessly insane Little Annie she was well and could go home. However, she didn't want to go. She wanted to stay and help others who were diagnosed as she had been.

You may recognize her name. Annie Sullivan. The same woman who later helped Helen Keller walk out of her darkness and into the light of a future. Helen and Annie inspired generations of people.

One elderly nurse, headed toward the end of her career, made a difference by sharing a few words, a little music, and some dessert. The hopelessly insane little girl who experienced love from that nurse, went on to impact a blind and deaf girl who changed the world.

15

When my Granny told me about the nurse and girl, I didn't fully understand it. I thought it was a great story, but when she told me the rest of the story, I never forgot it.

Granny said, "This one nurse's care and compassion had effectively changed the world. Think about it, Bubba. How many people did Ann Sullivan and Helen Keller impact during their lifetimes, and even today?"

Granny told me that there is no telling how many times our acts of kindness and compassion have changed the world—or at least the world for that person. And isn't that what life and grace are all about?

~

When we think about a life that matters, we often get lost in the big things, like a cure for a disease or a major social initiative. But what about the person who makes little steps or does little things for someone out of love? Doesn't this matter?

Doing little things was a big deal for Granny. She was continually doing something special for others.

Each act of love makes our lives matter in this broken world. You might not realize how your simple act of kindness and love is an answer to someone's prayer. We often don't know when we offer what little we have to someone who is hurting, how it is going to completely turn their life around.

Love is an action verb and it changes the world. You are a world-changer with your acts of caring, kindness, and love.

Your life matters!

Will you do something for me today?

I want you to look back on all the different times when you gave to a cause, helped someone in need, and did something that made a difference in someone else's life—no matter how large or small.

Write each one of them down. Take your time and list each one you can remember.

In the days to come, when you're feeling down, pull out that list and remember. Then that day, if possible, I want you to go out and do something for someone who cannot repay the favor. It will impact that person in ways that you can't begin to measure or know. It will also profoundly impact your life as well.

~

Mother Teresa's acts of love changed the world. She said,

"It is not how much we do,
but how much love we put in the doing.
It is not how much we give,
but how much love we put in the giving."

Mother Teresa

Mother Teresa was born in 1910 in Skopje, Macedonia. She realized at a young age that she had been called to be a nun. When she was eighteen, she joined a group of nuns in Ireland, the Sisters of Loreto.

After training for several months, she was granted permission to travel to India. She'd already heard of tremendous need and suffering among the people there. When she was twenty-one, she finalized her formal religious vows and chose to be named after Saint Therese of Lisieux, the patron saint of missionaries.

In India, she worked teaching children how to read, loving them with her whole heart. But she was struck by the profound poverty of the country and the people she served. She knew that she needed to do something more.

Mother Teresa prayed until God revealed what she needed to do. With that answer to her prayer, she started a new order called "The Missionaries of Charity".

The mission of their order was to serve the lowest of the low—who the caste system in India named "The Untouchables." Those were people that no one cared for or about. Under the Caste System rules, no one was to even look at "Untouchables."

Mother Teresa believed that serving others was fundamental to teaching them about Jesus Christ. "How can you reach them, if you don't serve them with His love first?"

She often spoke the words of Jesus, "Whatever you do to the least of my brethren, you do it to me."

"Love cannot remain by itself—it has no meaning.

Love has to be put into action,

and that action is service."

Mother Teresa

Even years later, after she had served for a long time, she tried to be the first person down to open the gates of the mission every morning. She said she wanted "to be there when Jesus showed up."

She looked for Jesus in each of their faces. What a beautiful mindset!

While she served the people of India, they endured the Bengal famine of 1943 and the Hindu/Muslim violence in 1946.

"In 1948, she left the convent to live full-time among the poorest of Calcutta. She chose to wear a white Indian sari, with a blue border, out of respect for the traditional Indian dress.

"For many years, Mother Teresa and a small band of fellow nuns survived on minimal income and food, often begging for funds. But, slowly her efforts with the poorest were noted and appreciated by the local community and Indian politicians.

"In 1952, she opened her first home for the dying, which allowed people to die with dignity. It afforded many neglected people the opportunity to die knowing that someone cared." (Pettinger, 2006)

News of her work spread around the world. By 2013, seven hundred missions were operating in over one hundred countries. The scope of their work expanded to include orphanages and hospices for those with terminal illnesses. (Pettinger, 2006)

"Not all of us can do great things.
But we can do small things with great love."

Mother Teresa

The Missionaries of Charity now have branches in the developed world where they work with the homeless and people affected by AIDS. By the mid-sixties, the organization became an International Religious Family by a decree of Pope Paul VI.

Mother Teresa was awarded the Nobel Peace Prize in 1979, "for work undertaken in the struggle to overcome poverty and distress, which also constitutes a threat to peace." (Pettinger, 2006)

When asked how to promote world peace, Mother Teresa replied, "Go home and love your family."

After her death, Pope John Paul, II formally beatified Mother Teresa in October 2003.

In September 2015, Pope Francis declared: "Mother Teresa, in all aspects of her life, was a generous dispenser of divine mercy, making herself available for everyone through her welcome and defense of human life, those unborn and those abandoned and discarded."

Pope John Paul wrote in his biography, "She bowed down before those who were spent, left to die on the side of the road, seeing in them their God-given dignity. She made her voice heard before the powers of this world so that they might recognize their guilt for the crime of poverty they created."

Mother Teresa did so much for the world and was an example to us all of how to give of ourselves to a cause greater than ourselves. But the key is that she was a simple woman who became committed to making a difference for those in need.

She was nothing special on her own. But her life mattered— not because of the masses to whom she brought comfort, but the one who was right in front of her at any given moment. Her life would have mattered even if she had only helped one person to a better life. I believe that is something we can all do and most likely already do.

Dr. Cliff Robertson, Jr.

Chapter 2

The Invisible Pain of Depression/Mental Health

Depression and mental health issues are rampant in our world today. I see it in my work as a counselor and in my capacity as founder of a veteran's homeless shelter. I live it every day.

As a pastor, I used to run a small group that focused on mental health, and it was the group with the highest attendance in the church. Statistics from the psychiatry.org website show that depression is an epidemic. About 17% of people walking around at any given time are suffering from depression

The National Institute of Mental Health (NIMH) statistics show that up to 25% of the world population suffers from a recognized anxiety disorder and yet, only about one-third of those are seeking any sort of treatment

When we are depressed, we feel like doing nothing. Or worse, we may feel like taking our own lives. We may feel like our lives are over or it will never get any better. We feel like our lives do not matter, but that is a lie.

There have been points in my life when I have struggled with depression. Sometimes it seemed so dark, I didn't know the way out. One day, in particular, a friend checked on me and I told her I was struggling.

She told me "Get out of the house. It's too beautiful a day to stay inside."

I wasn't sure what I was going to do but I went outside while we talked.

"Cliff, now drive to Wal Mart. When you get there buy a fall plant and give it to someone–anyone you see that might benefit from a little brightness in their day."

"Are you serious? You want me to go and buy a plant or flowers for someone I don't know and give it to them? They are going to think I'm crazy. They'll think I'm a stalker and just weird."

"Go and do it," she insisted.

Reluctantly, I got in my car and deliberately drove past the Wal-Mart near my home to a grocery store across town, hoping to avoid seeing anyone I knew. They'd certainly think I had lost my mind.

I took a deep breath and plodded inside. A beautiful display of fall plants greeted me near the entrance. At $10 each, I could do this. I looked over the plants, grabbed the first one I saw that looked decent, and headed for the checkout.

After I paid for the plant and headed out the exit door, I stood to the right to watch the people coming and going. How strange that no one looked at anyone else. It felt odd looking for the right person to give my gift to.

Where do I begin? How do I choose? Some people were dressed up and others dressed down. Then I spotted an elderly lady coming out of the store. She took short deliberate steps with her cart of groceries, focused on the asphalt in front of her. She pushed as if she were using all her strength to push a sled uphill.

I walked to her, smiled. "Hi, my name is Cliff, and I would like to give you this plant for your home and maybe if you would let me, help you to your car with these groceries."

She looked at me with a hint of a smile along with questions on her face. When she saw the plant in my hand, she lit up like a Christmas tree. "That's the nicest thing anyone ever offered to do for me."

I unloaded the groceries into her car and placed the plant in the seat next to her.

She gave me the biggest hug I had received in a long time and told me, "You absolutely made my day. Thank you so much."

For the first time in a while, a smile crept over my face. I told her, "You made a difference in my day too."

She tilted her head a little sideways with a question in her eyes, and then waved it off and thanked me again.

I'm not sure why I didn't tell her why I came and bought a gift for a stranger. Somehow it seemed like it might dim the beauty of the moment. It was enough for me to know that I had made a difference in someone's life. At that moment, it mattered more to me than I have words to express.

The depression that weighed me down, evaporated. It was a miracle to me. In fact, it felt so good, that I went back into the store and did it again and it was just as awesome the second time. I still do that from time to time.

By the way, I ended up marrying that friend who encouraged me to get out and give a gift to a stranger, but we'll get back to that later.

I have learned that when you do something for someone else who cannot repay you, it's as much a gift to you as it is to them.

This is all tied to a psychological theory called "Positive Psychology." We'll discuss this at length in the tool kit section of this book. Feel free to skip ahead and read it. It's important stuff.

Chapter 3

Your Life Matters—Even When You Have Made Bad Choices

My life has been a tough journey. At times it has been amazing and at other times it has been like a rocket ship on rails straight to hell.

I grew up in an alcoholic home. Mom was a true drunk. That led to other things, like cheating on my dad, stealing, and just not telling the truth. Hardly ever, telling the truth.

I remember one day when my sister and I were early junior high and late elementary school-aged. We were headed home from our grandfather's house with Mom, drunk, behind the wheel. Her driving was so erratic that my sister and I begged her to pull over and allow us to drive.

She finally did. I could only remember how scary it was when she was driving. However, many years later, my sister filled in the details of what happened after she pulled over. My sister reminded me that she had operated the foot pedals and I steered the car.

How we ever made it home safely that night, I have no idea. By the grace of God Almighty is all I know.

My parents divorced a few years later and that was a good thing. The arguments had gotten worse and worse. My dad even

27

warned me that separation was coming. I'm grateful he let me know.

What's amazing through all of this is that I never saw it as trauma. I just felt like it was normal, or at least not too unusual. I didn't feel bad for myself or about myself. I was just a boy playing sports, beginning to get interested in girls and living life.

Fast forward to adulthood. I went away to college and I married. We had a son, and I joined the military. I did my enlistment, experienced some success, and had some challenges.

When I got out, I struggled to find a job. I was on unemployment and it was tough to make ends meet. That Christmas, family friends helped buy presents for our now two children, Aaron and Chrystal.

Emotionally very low, I knew that I had to do something. So, without telling anyone, I left the house the next morning and promised myself I wasn't coming home until I got a job.

Armed with the local newspaper, and a couple of other job resources, I set off. As grace would have it, I got a job. A good job as a warehouse manager for a tire company.

With that job, I experienced some success and moved into sales. Later, I took a job with a bigger company. We moved just north of Houston, to the Conroe, Montgomery area. We found a place to live and got the kids settled into school.

All seemed well. Then one morning, I woke up with a horrible headache. Instead of going to work early, as usual, I decided to go back to bed. I got up in time to have breakfast with my family.

My wife's grandmother, Nana, had moved in with us to help us with the kids and to not be alone. She and my wife planned to take Chrystal to the doctor that day because she wasn't feeling well.

I dropped off Aaron at his school and went to work.

At work, I received a call from a prospective employer with an exciting new opportunity.

When I called my wife about the potential job, she was excited. "That's great! I'm about to take Chrystal to the doctor. Nana's coming too."

"Call me when you get back, and let me know how Chrystal is doing."

Back at my hectic office work, I made some phone calls to my customers. While I was on the office phone, I noticed a call come through on my cell phone that I didn't recognize, so I let it go to voicemail.

When I finished my phone call and checked my voicemail, a voice I didn't recognize left a message that there had been an accident.

My heart pounding, I immediately called him back. He answered, but I only picked up snippets of his words ... life-flight has just landed ... the accident is bad. He got my phone number from Nana, who was conscious but hurt ... a lot of pain.

A head-on collision with an eighteen-wheeler left Chrystal unresponsive but moaning in the backseat. Life Flight was summoned to take them to Hermann Memorial in downtown Houston.

I felt like I was in a scene from a movie and it couldn't be happening to me. I rushed to the hospital at warp speed, but there was nothing anyone could do.

I lost my wife that day and my daughter a week later.

I felt lost.

It seemed my life no longer had any purpose.

More than once I felt like killing myself to end the pain. The one thing that kept pulling me out of that downward spiral was my son, Aaron. What would happen to him?

One day, when the struggle was so intense, I couldn't stop the tears. Someone gave me a book and I tried to read some of it while I was parked in a Home Depot parking lot. The book only made me feel worse, so I threw the book out of my truck window.

It was pouring rain outside, and my tears flowed just as hard inside my truck. My vision was narrowed and all I could see was this ever-closing tunnel. I didn't know what to do or what was happening.

It was then that a memory sparked in my head. My wife and I used to shop at a Christian bookstore across the highway. Though I don't remember the drive, I ended up at that store and found a section about grief.

I thumbed through some of the books, not knowing where to look or even begin. But then I saw a name that I recognized, Dr. Luis Palau. I had heard him speak at a Promise Keepers convention years before. I picked up his book entitled *Where Is God When Bad Things Happen* and sat on the floor of that bookstore, reading his book. With his story of loss and the stories of others, I began to feel better.

One phrase, in particular, spoke to my grieving heart, "No matter how long or short a life may be, it is a complete life. Their life had had a God-Ordained purpose and meaning." There was something about that one phrase, that twenty years later, still rings in my soul. Life had a purpose and there was more to life than we could see or comprehend.

That book saved my life. It stopped my spiral but it did not fix me.

Even though I no longer considered ending my life, I still battled grief in ways that I didn't understand. I made really bad decisions including starting another relationship too soon, starting a new career, and a new business. While I experienced some success, it all failed. Thinking that it was tied to my proximity to where the accident occurred, I decided to move away.

But bad decisions, clouded with grief, all led to a downward spiral. A repeat of that "rocket ship on rails, headed straight to hell." I was a wreck.

At my lowest, I asked God to take my life. I told Him that my life was worthless and all I seemed to do was hurt people. I told Him that if I died, at least my new wife and kids would get some life insurance money. That was far better than I could do for them any other way.

I honestly felt like my life no longer mattered and my continued existence was making the planet worse.

Something happened though. God heard me but didn't answer my prayer with a "yes." He answered with, "I have something more for you."

At my rock bottom, I found Jesus and it changed me. With that, everything began to change. Initially, the change was on the inside of me. I began to study, learn, and see hope, even though I didn't know what all that looked like at the time.

I worked on a degree in Biblical Studies, then a Masters in Divinity, and finally a Doctorate in Theology. Writing came to me as a calling, and I wrote like a man on fire.

I share this with you to let you know that life, even at the very bottom is not over. On my journey, I was blessed to have the opportunity to serve many along the way. I counseled and spoke most every week. I helped people with language barriers write letters. I wrote pardon applications and appeals for people. I was able to make a difference for many.

Life can be tough. There are times when you feel worthless, and that there is no purpose. But trust me, as long as you are breathing you have a purpose.

But that is only part of the story.

I came to realize that when we impact a person's life for the good, we impact everyone they come in contact with - from their family, the place they work, and the neighborhood they live in. The list could go on and on.

When we find ways to bless others every day, we can literally change the world, one person and positive act at a time.

George Mueller

In college, I studied about George Mueller. He became one of my heroes. If you haven't heard of him, Mueller built great orphanages on simple faith. Eventually, these orphanages covered thirteen acres of land on Ashley Downs, in Bristol, England. But, when God put it into the heart of George Mueller to build these orphanages, George had only two shillings (fifty cents) in his pocket.

By the time of Mr. Muller's death, there were five immense buildings of solid granite, capable of accommodating two thousand orphans. Without making his desires known to anyone but God, over one million, four hundred thousand pounds ended up being donated – over seven million U.S. dollars today. It arrived as it was needed, to build and maintain the orphanages.

Although George Mueller became famous as one of the greatest men of prayer known to history, he was not always a saint. He wandered into a deep mess before he came to Christ.

Mueller was born in Prussia, in 1805. His father was a tax collector. Not the best example for a young man, his father spent much of his time in the bars and brothels.

George routinely lied to his father about the money he spent, both how much he spent and where he threw it away. He also stole from his father when his father was drunk or out spending time with the women in the brothels.

Since his father was wrapped up in the dark side of the world, he didn't provide much fatherly instruction. He gave the family money, that they quickly burned through. At ten years of age, George was sent to a Christian school. His father wanted to make a Lutheran clergyman of him, not that he might serve God, but that he might have an easy and comfortable living wage from the State Church. (Lawson, 1911).

"My time," said George, "was now spent in studying, reading novels, and indulging … in sinful practices. Thus, it continued until I was fourteen years old when my mother suddenly died. The night she was dying, I, not knowing of her illness, was playing cards until two in the morning. On the next day, being the Lord's Day, I went with some of my companions to a tavern, and then, being filled with strong beer, we went about the streets drunk."

"I grew worse and worse," said Mueller. "Three or four days before I was confirmed (and thus admitted to partake of the Lord's supper), I was guilty of gross immorality; and the very day before my confirmation, when I was in the vestry with the clergyman to confess my sins (according to the usual practice), after a formal manner, I defrauded him; for I handed over to him only a twelfth part of the fee which my father had given me for him."

Lying, stealing, gambling, skirt-chasing, wasteful spending, was just the tip of the iceberg. No one would have imagined that this wayward young soul would become known for his faith in God and his power in prayer.

When his father sent young George to collect rent, George would lie about the amount he collected and pocket the difference. His reckless behavior brought him to the point of having no money to buy food. He even stole bread from a soldier.

In 1821, George went to Magdeburg and spent six days there drinking and chasing women. From there, he went to Brunswick and rented an expensive hotel until his money ran out. Next, he rented a room at a fine hotel in a neighboring village, intending to defraud the hotel. Caught before he could leave, he traded his finest clothes for rent money. He then walked six miles to another inn, where he was arrested for trying to defraud the landlord. (Lawson, 1911). This time he was jailed for his crime, at sixteen years old.

But then something that can only be described as a "come to Jesus" moment occurred in his life. While at school, one of his friends brought him to the house of a Christian family on a Saturday afternoon.

They ate dinner together and afterward began a Bible study that was far deeper than any he had been involved in before. His heart was moved in a way he had never experienced. Before George could ask a question of the man leading the study, the man quietly slipped to his knees to pray, and his family joined him in prayer.

George had never experienced this, even in all the Christian Studies and seminary/clergyman schooling he had attended. George, unsure what to do, joined them on his knees, too.

In that moment of solemn prayer, George surrendered his life to Christ. He began to cry for the errors of his ways and wanted to do nothing but make amends and share the love of Christ with everyone he came in contact with. It was a moment of real transformation.

He went on to preach around the countryside and then moved to London to preach there. In 1834, Mr. Mueller started the Scripture Knowledge Institution for Home and Abroad to aid Christian day-schools, assist missionaries, and circulate the Scriptures.

Shortly after this, he began the orphanages that impacted so many children. "These institutions of both learning and housing, without government support, without asking anyone for help, without contracting debts; without committees, subscribers, or memberships; but through faith in the Lord alone and intense prayer, had raised and disbursed no less a sum than £1,500,000 ($7,500,000) at the time of Mr. Mueller's death." (Lawson, 1911). The bulk of this was spent on the orphanage.

"By the time Mueller died, 122,000 persons had been taught in the schools supported by these funds; and about 282,000 Bibles and 1,500,000 Testaments had been distributed through the same fund. Also, 112,000,000 religious books, pamphlets, and tracts had been circulated; missionaries had been aided in all parts of the world, and no less than ten thousand orphans had been cared for using this same fund." (Lawson, 1911).

At the age of seventy, Mr. Mueller made great evangelistic tours, traveling 200,000 miles around the world. He preached in many lands and several different languages, frequently speaking to as many as 4,500 to 5,000 people.

He preached three to four times throughout the United States. He continued his evangelistic tours until he was ninety years of age. During these seventeen years of evangelistic work, he estimated he had addressed three million people. All his expenses had been paid by those who sent in funds, in answer to his prayers of faith.

It would be an understatement to say that George Mueller's life mattered, but I am struck by the times when there was neither food nor money to buy food. As mealtimes in the orphanages drew near, they gathered around the tables in the dining hall and George prayed. All the staff and children would file in and they would join him silently praying.

They were always interrupted by a knock on the door. Someone would deliver food saying, "I felt moved by the Lord to bring this to your institution. I hope it helps."

No one had said a word publicly, other than their prayers to God. No one had cried in the streets for help or set up a fundraising drive. They prayed.

This wasn't an isolated occurrence. If that were the case, many would think it to be a coincidence. But their prayers were answered every time there was a need or a shortage.

Every time.

No one ever went without a meal in these orphanages, ever.

I wonder about the impact that this type of devoted prayer must have had on the people at the orphanages who witnessed it, from the staff to the residents. How did this shape their lives of faith?

I imagine it had a tremendous impact on them. Simply learning about the story has had a profound impact on me.

So, you see, your past does not define your future. You can begin again today and live in such a way that the change inspires others and leads them out of their darkness. "If I did it, so can you," will be your byline. Then you reach down and lift them up and walk with them a while.

Chapter 4

Disability & Its Many Forms

One of the greatest challenges that anyone faces is a reduction in their physical or mental capacity to perform the things that others take for granted. We feel like we are somehow less, and therefore we become depressed and even feel hopeless, not to mention helpless. According to the CDC, one person in every four in America suffers from some sort of disability or chronic illness.

When we allow this to define our story, I believe that we lose something very important – that we were made for a purpose.

Dana S. Dunn, Ph.D., and Shane Burcaw wrote, "In psychological research, the term "identity" is often used to refer to the self, expressions of individuality, and the groups to which people belong. Our identities define us because they contain personality traits and highlight social roles, and they can be focused on our past, present, and future selves. Disability is a particular identity context, one that marks individuals as part of a group and as members of a minority sometimes subjected to marginalization, prejudice, or discrimination. "Disability identity" refers to possessing a positive sense of self and feelings of connection to, or solidarity with, the disability community.

Coherent disability identity is believed to help individuals adapt to a disability, including navigating related social stresses and daily hassles."

Let that resonate inside your soul for a moment. You are not alone in your disability. You have strengths and gifts that are unique to you and a purpose that is solely yours.

Dr. Dunn also wrote, "Identities help people make sense of different and distinct parts of their self-concepts. For people with disabilities, an identity should contain relevant content and goals linked to disability. In effect, "disability identity" should guide people with disabilities towards what to do, what to value, and how to behave in those situations where their disability stands out, as well as those where it is not salient."

To better understand what the good doctor meant, I want to share a couple of stories that speak about this.

Joni Eareckson Tada is a good example. She grew up in an active family that spent a lot of time outdoors and in athletic endeavors. Her father was an Olympic athlete, and the family practically lived outdoors. Growing up in Baltimore, Joni often swam and camped along the Chesapeake.

One summer day she decided to dive from a rock perched pretty high above the water. She ran as fast as she could and dove out, executing a perfect swan dive. Her dive felt like a dream come true, feeling like she was floating as much as flying. She hoped to land the dive in true Olympic form, with a minimal splash.

But the water hit her like a brick wall. She had a momentary flash of intense pain just after entering the water and then nothing. Nothing at all. Something was wrong. She didn't feel anything, and nothing worked. She couldn't move her hands, her arms, her legs.

When her family didn't see her come up right away, they went in the water after her. They retrieved her limp body from the water and cleared the water from her lungs. Someone ran to get help and the ambulance arrived soon.

Joni went from an active seventeen-year-old girl to a quadriplegic in less than a second. As you might imagine, she struggled with this new reality. In that hospital bed she faced suicidal despair, extreme depression, and to top it all off, she felt like God had abandoned her. Even though she was a woman of faith, she did not understand how God could allow this to happen. She just wanted it to be over.

It seemed like everyone had a religious platitude of the day for her. Rather than inspire her, it made her sick of anything to do with God or Christianity.

But then one day during occupational therapy, she learned that she could use her mouth to hold a paintbrush and paint. Her faith began to come back to her as she painted images of heaven. Her paintings were so good, people wanted to buy them.

But selling paintings was not the end of Joni's work. She also learned to use her mouth to write her story. It became a best seller and was made into a movie. She continued to write about seventy more books.

It is funny to hear her husband, Ken, talk about Joni and their first date. He was nervous. He was a football coach/teacher and she was a famous Christian author, artist, and speaker.

When he described her, he never mentioned her disabilities. Did he not recognize them?

Of course, he did. But there is an important lesson for us here.

The right person in your life,

sees you first

and then sees your challenges/disabilities

as an opportunity

to serve and love you more.

From her perspective, she worried what he would think and if he was prepared for life, or even a date, with a quadriplegic. She learned quickly, that he was not easily deterred. Even having to change a colostomy bag on a first date did not dissuade him from the love of his life.

Joni Eareckson Tada has faced many challenges in her life, many of which most people could not even begin to grasp. She could have given up on life and almost did.

Once she saw some light, in the form of a new gift for painting, her life began to turn around. While her circumstances did not change, she began to change. Her paintings, music, books, speaking, and movies, have touched millions around the world for over forty years.

She started a non-profit to help those with disabilities. The Joni and Friends Disability Center helps those in need. She has a radio program, Joni and Friends, that goes out over a thousand different stations.

Even when she thought her life was over, her life still mattered more than she could even begin to grasp. Consider the following statement.

She has impacted more people throughout her life,

due to her disability,

than most people who have no disability

could ever hope for.

I wonder about you right now. According to statistics, there is a 25% or better chance that you suffer from a disability or chronic illness. It could be something simple or incredibly complex. There could be a cure, or not. The truth is that you are uniquely gifted for a mission in this life. While it is pretty easy to recognize that Joni's life matters, I want you to know that so does yours.

So, what is your story? Maybe you need to write it down.

What is your gift? Sometimes we get so down in a dark place that we cannot see the gifts that are right in front of our faces. When we get to that place, a feeling of hopelessness sets in.

I want you to know that the dark places in our minds can be overcome. Know that you are not alone and that as long as there is breath in your lungs, there is hope for a better future.

Helen Keller

What happened to babies who contracted meningitis in the 1880s?

Most of them died.

One nineteen-month-old little girl defied the odds and survived the disease, but lost her sight and hearing. Her parents didn't know how to help, but Helen found a way to communicate using hand signals. The first person to recognize her signals was the family maid/cook, Martha.

By the time she was seven, Helen had created over sixty hand signs that enabled her to communicate with family and friends. She could tell who was there by the vibration of their steps.

But during this era, this still gave Helen very little hope of a fulfilling life. Her parents knew that they would be taking care of her for the rest of their lives, a burden they would gladly take. But still, in their quiet moments, they wondered why God would allow such things to happen.

Her mother never gave up on her though. Even though they didn't have a lot of money, she continued to search for options that might give her little girl some sense of a normal life. She read the book, *American Notes,* by Charles Dickens about a deaf and blind girl getting a real education and that inspired her even more.

After a visit with Alexander Graham Bell, who was working with the deaf, and a referral to the Perkins Institute for the Blind, they finally found a place that might help. There, a young woman, an alumnus of their program, worked with young Helen.

This began a fifty-year journey for the two of them. They spanned the globe together. With her helper, Helen graduated from Radcliffe, which eventually merged with Harvard. Helen wrote fourteen books and spoke around the world.

The young girl from the Perkins Institute for the Blind, who became Helen's companion for fifty years was Anne Sullivan—the same "Crazy Annie", we learned about earlier.

These women changed the world and still have an impact on it today. I wonder how many people these ladies helped, either directly or indirectly, by their example?

The numbers are most likely staggering. This in turn makes me wonder how many books were written, jobs created and inventions patented due to their work and influence on others?

There is no way to fully understand or comprehend the totality of it all. I wonder what impact they may have had on Mr. Bell? I wonder how many other areas of life their impact reached?

This all makes me sit back in wonder of how much we matter, even when everything around us seems to be hopeless. We can never fully grasp how much our daily contributions to this world impact it for good, but we can rest assured that the difference is significant.

Your life matters.

Stop and think about it. Total it up and see for yourself. You might be surprised at the total of your importance on this planet.

When I think about this concept, I wonder how many people are reading this, who suffer from disabilities, who may be considering ending their lives?

I know that it is a very real topic. According to research at the NIH, suicide among those with disabilities and chronic illness is much higher than among the general population. The rates of depression are much higher as well. Many give up and think that life simply isn't worth it.

But I want you to know something. You have great value. Your life matters.

You might think, "My life will never compare to these two you have mentioned. I will never make a difference."

I will tell you they are not the only ones. There are people every day struggling with disabilities and chronic illness that are changing the world in small and large ways."

~

I love the story of Sarah Young who writes devotionals. She has changed many lives for the good but you will never hear her in an interview. She only gives interviews by email. Some call her a recluse, but according to an interview in Publishers Weekly, she has suffered from some pretty severe illnesses, associated with Lyme disease, that made her life pretty tough (Butcher, 2012).

According to the article, her writing was inspired by her illness and the hope that she found in Christ through it (Butcher, 2012). She hoped her writing might help someone else who found themselves in a dark place and bring them the hope that Christ brought her (Butcher, 2012).

You may think, I am not a writer. I can't do what she does. Maybe you are right, but have you tried?

I also want to introduce you to another lady. Her name is Karen. She suffers from a hereditary neuromuscular disease— CMT, Charcot-Marie-Tooth. CMT begins when your nerve endings die, and this slowly makes it impossible to walk or do things with your hands. It can also affect your breathing. While it is not fatal by itself, it can certainly create problems that can lead to death.

If you were to meet Karen, you would not know that she had a disability, until it was time for her to walk. She would look you in the eye and give you her undivided attention. She would engage with you and ask questions, truly wanting to know you. She would make you think that you are the most important person in the world to her, and at that moment, you would be. She treats all of her friends that way.

She grew up not knowing why she was different. Her mother had CMT as well, but it was never diagnosed. Karen just knew that there were things that she couldn't do, like run and jump, swim, and climb. Those things took muscle coordination and strength that CMT had taken from her. But she was a determined young lady, so she went to college and studied hard. She became a special education teacher and was highly sought after. Then she went on to teach the gifted and talented in a small school in East Texas called, Coldspring.

She was one of those special teachers who students remember forever. The kind that affects your life so it is forever changed for the better because you met her. She helped hundreds of young minds see the possibilities beyond their circumstances. She helped them to see their inner brilliance unlike anyone else in their lives ever had. She was voted teacher of the year for the local school and the region but she often turned it down. She never wanted to draw attention to herself. Her disability made her feel unworthy.

Years later, many of her students are still in contact with her and write to her about the difference that she made in their lives.

I think about this one woman, who was able to touch the minds, hearts, and lives of so many. She helped them to believe that anything was possible. I think that people with disabilities have been given special gifts. They see things differently and recognize the struggles of others. They are often more empathetic and know how to make others shine.

Karen still makes people she spends time with feel like they are the most important people in the world. I am the lucky man blessed to spend my life with this amazing woman. She is my wife.

She is the one, who before we got married or were even dating, told me to get out of the house when I was down. She encouraged me to go give away a plant to someone at Wal Mart. She is the one, who on her birthday, when we had gone out to eat at our favorite place, looked around the room and said, "Honey, for my birthday, I want us to buy that man, sitting over there by himself, dinner without him knowing that it was us."

That not only made me not just smile, but I realized that she was slowly but surely changing the world one act of kindness at a time. She inspires me every day. I am blessed.

By the way, the man at the restaurant looked around the place smiling, not knowing who it was. He will likely never forget that night. He will also, more than likely, turn around and do the same for someone else or some other act of kindness that makes this world a little better.

Have you heard of "The Butterfly Effect?" It's the theory that when something happens—like a butterfly flapping its wings in one part of the world—it affects the winds in another part of the world, like a ripple on a pond.

What if, even during your greatest challenges, you set out to be like the butterfly flapping your wings? What if doing something for someone else that makes them smile, helps them see their life has meaning?

It changes the world for that person and it gives your life meaning as well.

#YourLifeMatters

Dr. Cliff Robertson, Jr.

Chapter 5

Socio-Economic Status—I'm broke. I grew up poor. So how can my life matter?

Depression and anxiety are the two most common things Americans struggle with. Sometimes this is caused by a chemical imbalance that requires medication to help a person work through it and thrive. Other times, it is because of circumstances such as the ones listed below.

- Grief over the loss of a loved one or the loss of a significant relationship.
- Financial distress. Loss of job, loss of a capacity to earn, stock market losses.
- Persistent feelings of failure and shame.
- Feeling like, "I don't measure up. I'm not good enough. I'm not smart enough. I'm too poor."
- Bullying. Being bullied or shamed into doing things.
- Disability. Serious medical condition. Terminal or chronic illness.
- Legal trouble. Criminal or civil.
- Adverse childhood. Trauma/ abuse/ neglect.

- Discrimination.

You may remember the staggering statistics from chapter 2 with 25% of Americans dealing with anxiety and/or depression in one form or another at any given moment.

So what does this mean? Why does this matter? Why are we even talking about it?

When I look at those numbers, I see the hurt and the pain associated with it. So many have lost their loved ones and friends and they are wondering why they are still here.

"Why do I exist?"

"I have no purpose. All I do is hurt. I can't pay my bills. Why should I even live?"

Many people ask that question. When they have no answer, they choose to die by suicide. It has become the tenth leading cause of death in America today, taking around 50,000 lives each year.

I'd like to tell you a story about a woman who you might not have heard about. She grew up poor, one of twenty-four children, and a minority in Detroit.

She married at thirteen to escape problems at home and it didn't end well. Her husband was an alcoholic and a bigamist, and he left her with two young boys and no support.

She worked two and three jobs at a time to make ends meet. With no formal education, she cleaned floors, homes, and bathrooms—whatever work she could find.

That was a hard life already. Add the responsibility of two young boys, who would often go unsupervised for hours at a time, in tough neighborhoods. This created a nearly hopeless situation. She was stern with them and made them study and read. They couldn't turn on the TV until after all their homework was complete.

During that time, she was struck with clinical depression.

Instead of allowing her challenges with depression to drag her and her boys down, she got the help she needed. Family members took care of the boys for a couple of months until she came back home.

She could have let that stigma of mental illness drag her down and keep her there, but she didn't. She went back to work and instilled the same work ethic and overcoming spirit into her boys. This mom had her sons read books that opened their minds and encouraged them to study hard. She cared about them and worked to make a difference in their lives every day. She did the very best she could.

Her life mattered because she didn't give up, even when she had to be so tired - physically, emotionally, and spiritually. And yet, each day she got up and did all she could one more day. Isn't that what we are all called to do?

Her story of struggle isn't unique. Her uncommon courage is. She defied the odds and not only survived but thrived – and so did her boys.

One son worked hard and earned excellent grades. He became a mechanical engineer.

The other son wanted to become a doctor. A brain surgeon, better known as a neurosurgeon. That son earned his Pre-Med degree from Yale and went to the University of Michigan for medical school.

He has now written best-selling books. A movie has been made about his life. He has run for President of the United States and was appointed to be the 17th Secretary of Housing and Urban Development, Dr. Ben Carson.

His mother's name was Sonya Carson, and her life mattered.

At any point in her life, she could have given up. Many others have given up, but not Ms. Carson. People throw up their hands every day, and walk away from families, abandoning children. They just quit on life. But not her.

When she battled clinical depression while working three jobs, she might have asked, "Is this all there is?"

But she didn't let that stop her. I believe her faith allowed her to see, that even during times of great struggles, there was still hope.

That's how Sonya Carson lived her life. She didn't know how her boys were going to turn out but she was determined to give them all she had.

She was changing the world by loving her sons.

Each day that she invested in those boys yielded a change in the world for the better.

Her story could be your story too. We each make an impact on this world.

Each day matters. It is a gift.

#YourLifeMatters.

Oseola McCarty, a washerwoman

What is a "washerwoman" and how could she change the world? A washerwoman went to someone's home and washed their clothes. Hanging, folding, and ironing them as needed.

This was a very low-paying job, but for someone who has no formal education and is willing to work hard, it helped to pay the bills.

Meet Ms. Osceola McCarty. When she was a young girl, Osceola's aunt became ill and could not take care of herself. This led Osceola to leave school to take care of her sick aunt. After that, she did what other women in her family had done for years – she became a washerwoman.

She was very frugal and saved all the money she could. She opened an account at TrustMark Bank in Hattiesburg Mississippi. When she earned money from her work, she deposited it there.

She didn't own a car, preferring to walk everywhere she went. She didn't subscribe to the newspaper, thinking it an extravagance. She had a black and white television and only watched the broadcast shows through the major networks.

Oseola was diligent about saving money in her bank account. As her account grew, the bankers at TrustMark bank noticed, and wanted to make sure that she was taken care of. They started working on her behalf as unofficial guardians. They convinced her to buy a couple of window air-conditioner units, and some other things for her personal welfare.

Then one day, when she was coming into the bank to make her routine deposit, one of the trust officers stopped and warmly greeted Ms. McCarty. He called her by name and invited her to his office. He also called in a man she knew well... An attorney she did laundry for.

At first, she was concerned that there might be a problem.

The bank trust officer quickly put her mind at ease. Nothing was wrong. This was a good meeting. He just wanted to share some good news with her. He asked her, "Oseola, do you know how much money you have in the bank?"

She said, "No, why don't you tell me?"

"Well, Oseola, you have over $250,000 in your account."

"I don't know if that is a lot of money or not, sir."

"Oseola, it is a lot of money and I would like to know what you would like to do with all of your money. Let me explain." He took out ten dimes and some slips of paper. He explained to her that each dime would represent 10% of her total. Each slip of paper would represent where she wanted that money to go.

She looked at the two men, smiled, and said, "This is a blessing isn't it!" Then she reached over to the first dime and said, "I want this to go my church."

The trust officer wrote the name of Friendly Baptist Church on the slip.

Then Oseola reached over and moved the second, third and fourth dimes over and said, "I would like for this to go to my three remaining relatives." She then gave the names to the trust officer.

She looked at the remaining six and said, "I want the rest of this to go for a scholarship at University Southern Mississippi, to students that are not otherwise going to be able to go to school, preferably of African American descent."

The attorney put together the trust document and the bank helped to manage her money for the rest of her life.

When the word got out, that a washerwoman had just given over $250,000 away, and mostly for a scholarship, local leaders in the Hattiesburg area founded an endowment in her honor to make sure that this gift would be recognized forever.

President Bill Clinton awarded Oseola McCarty the Presidential Citizens award. The University of Southern Mississippi awarded her its first honorary degree. Then Harvard followed up giving her an Honorary Doctorate.

The founder of CNN, Ted Turner, said, "I'm inspired. If a washerwoman can give away all she has, maybe I need to step up to the plate as well. I pledge a billion dollars of my fortune to causes around the world."

A lot of people stepped up and contributed because of this one woman's story. But as a closing note, Oseola wanted just one thing—to see the person who received the first scholarship walk across the stage.

She was afraid, that because of her advanced age and poor health that this might not happen. In 1999, the first graduate of the Oseola McCarty Scholarship walked across the stage at USM, and Oseola was there.

She passed away several months later from complications related to cancer. A reporter sought out the scholarship recipient who graduated and asked her to comment on the passing of her benefactor.

She was quoted as saying, "The world is such a better place because of Oseola McCarty. She brought sunshine everywhere she went and asked for nothing in return. And now heaven is even brighter with their newest angel."

There is so much to say here, but just let this story settle into your heart.

Think, what is possible for me?

How much of a difference can I make in this world if I will just commit to making daily efforts for the good?

Chapter 6
Loss/Grief/Tragedy

There are two types of people in this world when it comes to loss, grief, and tragedy—those who have experienced it and those who will. It is inevitable.

The impact of these losses, regardless of how inevitable they may be, can generate so much pain and anguish that many people lose the will to live through it. Some people have died of a broken heart after the loss of a loved one.

The saying goes that grief will lessen over time as we learn to move on. But sometimes it doesn't go away. It becomes chronic grief that only gets worse.

A personal note from me-if this is how you are feeling, then I want you to put this book down and call a mental health professional today, preferably one who specializes in grief. This is important. Please do it.

When someone is experiencing grief over loss—whether from a loved one who lost their battle with a disease, or a sudden tragedy where their life was taken unexpectedly—it is always filled with intense emotional pain. It can feel overwhelming and leave you in a place where you are not sure where to turn or what to do next.

When I reflect on my story and the loss of my wife and little girl in the car accident, I still feel some remnants of that pain, even though it happened over twenty years ago. I say that to let you know that the wound heals but the scars remain and so do their precious memories.

During the pain of the loss, I struggled immensely. After their funerals, I spent two weeks on the couch.

I couldn't sleep in the bedroom where my wife and I slept. I only went into that room for a shower and to change clothes. That was all I could manage.

While in that pit of grief, my sister and a friend of hers came over one day, completely unannounced. They told me they were there to clean up my house and pack away Barbara and Chrystal's things. They would donate them to a battered women's shelter.

I am forever grateful for what they did that day. It forced me off the couch and was a little bit of a push that helped me to rejoin life.

But I still struggled. A lot.

Remember the day I wrote about earlier when I was in the parking lot? I threw a book out the window of my truck and I ended up at a Christian bookstore reading the Dr. Luis Palau book, *Where Is God, When Bad Things Happen*?

You may remember that I sat down on the floor by the book racks and got lost in the book and the stories he shared. I am pretty sure that I read and cried for over two hours. His statement stuck with me. *"Every life no matter how long or short is a complete life. Their life had had a God-ordained purpose and meaning."*

It was that statement—that truth—that allowed me to be able to move forward. You see, at that moment, all I could see was the pain. All I could hear were my questions. "Why did God take my wife and my daughter? They were both so young and filled with so much life.

Why didn't he take me instead?

Why?

I had so many questions but no answers. I believe God used the statement in that book to save my life. Up to that point, I had contemplated suicide several times. After that truth pierced my heart, I knew that I couldn't go through with it. I wasn't able to explain it all then, but I just knew.

I got up off the floor of the bookstore, walked to the counter, and paid for the book. The sales clerk wasn't sure what to say to me. I'm sure in my emotional state, I looked a mess, and she wondered if I was okay. Her face showed me her concern, but she didn't ask questions. She took my money, gave me my change, and tried to put the book in a bag. I said it wasn't necessary and walked out of the store to drive home.

One of the stories that rang so true in my heart was the story that Dr. Luis Palau shared about the loss of a little girl. Of course, that story resounded in my own heart because of the loss of my daughter.

Dr. Palau, an international evangelist, was in England to speak at a week-long revival. The first couple of nights, he noticed a little girl in the audience. She listened intently each night. On the third night she came down front, and while speaking with a female counselor, gave her heart to Christ.

Dr. Palau made it part of his routine to come down front and greet each person who made a decision for Christ. He looked the little girl in the eyes and told her that he loved her and that Jesus loved her even more.

The little girl asked him to pray for her father who was an alcoholic and didn't believe. Dr. Palau prayed with the little girl and then moved on to the next person.

The revival was a huge success and his scheduled one-week revival stretched into two weeks. The little girl kept coming but she was always by herself. Her father never came with her.

One night on her walk home from the evening's revival, tragedy struck. The girl was hit by a car and died instantly. It was an accident. A dark road. The driver said he never saw the little girl until it was too late. The whole town mourned. Dr. Palau learned that the little girl had died on her way home from the revival.

He set out to find where she lived, and to see her father. He hoped to bring him some comfort but he couldn't be sure of the welcome he would get. When he found the home, he saw garbage bins overflowing with empty whiskey bottles.

I imagine the story playing out something like this –

Dr. Palau knocked on the door and the man inside screamed for whoever it was to go away.

Dr. Palau knocked on the door again, speaking this time, "I am Luis Palau, the evangelist. I met your daughter at the revival meetings down the road. I know this has to be hard. I want to see if I can be of any help."

No screaming came this time, just the sound of footsteps coming closer to the door. The door swung open and the man said "I have been wanting to speak to you."

Dr. Palau walked in the door and the man pointed at a chair. They both sat down. The smell of alcohol and something not quite identifiable filled the air. It was most likely remains of rotting food.

The little girl's father stared at the evangelist for a while and the silence was deafening. Dr. Palau began to speak, and the father held his hand up to stop him.

He said, "You killed my little girl. It is all your fault. If you hadn't been here and been preaching all that nonsense, selling her a bill of goods, she would have never been out on that dark night. She would still be with us. It is your fault and I hold you personally responsible!"

The man cried out in anger and anguish. When he stopped raging, he slumped in his chair, as if he had said his peace and officially given up. He reached over to the small table next to his chair for the next bottle of whiskey.

Before he could open it, Dr. Palau spoke. "Dear sir, I know that you must blame me. If I were you, I would blame me, too. The pain over the loss of a child is beyond what most can imagine. I have not lost a child, but I have lost a father at a young age. I know the pain of loss.

"I got to meet your little girl on the fourth night of the revival. Before that night, I noticed her in the crowd. Such a beautiful child. When she came down front and spoke with one of our female Christian counselors, she prayed to receive Christ in her heart and she was so full of life and hope. That night, after the service, I went down front and met with each of those who made that decision. When I got to her, she told me about her father. How she loved him but that he wouldn't come, and that he drank a lot. She was genuinely worried about you and asked if we could pray for you. And we did.

The father had set the bottle down on the floor now, crying, almost uncontrollably. He said, "She prayed for me and asked you to join her?"

Dr. Palau, continued, "She did. We both prayed for you."

The father muttered, "I thought she hated me. She was always getting onto me for drinking. I would scream at her to leave me alone and she'd run away crying. I was such a horrible father … and she prayed for me? What kind of monster I must be … I can't do this. You need to leave, so I can get my affairs in order."

Knowing that the term "affairs in order" did not mean cleaning up the house, Dr. Palau resolved to see this through. He said, "We prayed—both she and I, that you would be freed from the grip of alcohol and its destructiveness, and become gripped by the grace of Jesus Christ, knowing that you have an eternal home in heaven when your life comes to an end. Experiencing the joy of His love here and His eternal joy and love in heaven."

This hit the man like a ton of bricks. He stopped crying, sat up in his chair, leaned forward, and asked, "My little girl is with Jesus?"

"Yes," was the quick answer from Dr. Palau.

The father said, "I need help because I cannot live another day knowing that I will never again see my little girl. Can you help me?"

Dr. Palau got down on his knees in this man's house and invited him to join him. He explained that Christ had died for him and rose on the third day, that we might have eternal life if we will just believe. That this is a choice—a decision that will forever change your life. One day, when you pass away, you will see your daughter again. He quoted the passage where David said of his baby that died, "Can I bring him back again? I shall go to him, but he shall not return to me." 2 Samuel 12:23

Dr. Palau led this bereaved father in the same prayer that his daughter prayed when she gave her heart to Christ. The men knelt there on the floor and embraced in a flood of tears.

The father asked if it would be okay if he attended the revival meeting that night.

Dr. Palau said, "Of course."

He also asked if Dr. Palau would say a few words at the little girl's funeral the next day.

Dr. Palau responded that he would be honored.

The man got up and said, "I need to get this place cleaned up. I need to get ready for tonight and tomorrow."

Dr. Palau asked, "Can I help?"

The man said, with the first of many smiles, "Dear sir, you have done more than enough. I will see you tonight." And he did.

The man came down front, to the astonishment of the entire community. Everyone knew he was a drunkard and the story about his daughter's death. His response led others to make decisions, too. The altar was full that night.

In the end, Dr. Palau came down front and gave the man a big hug. They both cried again. The next day, Dr. Palau attended the funeral and said a few words. He told the story, and more came to know Christ that night on the last night of the revival.

The father not only cleaned up his house but his life. His life was so completely transformed that those who knew him before could hardly recognize him afterward. Those who just met him could not believe that he had been the town drunk. He helped others at every opportunity. He attended church regularly, and his drinking days were over.

There is more to this story than we will likely never know this side of heaven, but we rest assured that God promises He works all things together for the good, for those that love Him and are called according to His purpose (paraphrase of Romans 8:28). In other words, God will take a tragedy and bring about miracles that are beyond our capacity of reason.

Remember, your life matters.

Maybe your greatest struggles will lead you to your greatest triumphs. How inspiring it will be when someone tells you, "I want to do what you have done."

I know I have heard that statement several times. It is just a reminder that the things we do really matter. We might be the inspiration someone else needs to come to Christ, turn their life around, and change their own world. This will, in turn, change the world around them.

It's not surprising this isn't the only story of loss that turned out to be a miracle.

Mordecai Ham & Billy Graham

No matter where you go in this world, you've probably heard of Billy Graham.

But many of us may have never heard the name Mordecai Ham or Mordecai's parents, Tobias and Ollie Ham. The stories of their lives are not well known at all, and yet, they were incredibly instrumental in the journey of millions of people hearing the gospel all around this world from a North Carolina called Billy.

Mordecai Ham was a traveling evangelist from Kentucky who was called to ministry at the early age of nine years old. (McDaniel, 2018). He was best remembered for a revival he preached in North Carolina, leading a sixteen-year-old Billy Graham to Christ.

Tobias and Ollie Ham, Mordecai's parents, raised him to know and honor the Lord. How amazing that we never know when or how the fruit of our labors will be revealed. We can trust that if we are planting well, a good harvest will come.

Speaking of harvest, Mordecai's parents were farmers. American farm life was hard in the 1800s. I wonder if his mother, Ollie, ever thought her life mattered. Seeing after her children, husband, and constant challenges that life throws at you on a little farm in Kentucky could certainly have caused her to grow weary and to lose hope.

I wonder if Mordecai's father, Tobias Ham, a dedicated man of God, ever wished he could have a bigger church, or have bigger crowds on Sunday mornings. While we can never know the answers to these questions, we do know that they loved and served God with all they had. We do know they were faithful in the things God gave them. Life on that Kentucky farm and in their little country church wasn't easy but it was all a gift and they cherished it. They planted more than crops on that farmland. They planted God's word into the hearts of their children and all that would listen on Sunday morning.

Life on the farm and in the ministry had to be tough, and there was no money. The great depression had hit the rest of the world, but as the saying goes, "they were so poor they couldn't tell." They were so poor, in fact, that as Mordecai Ham witnessed his family's financial struggles—often going to bed hungry and wearing hand-me-down clothes that never fit—he became convinced that the hard farm life and that of a preacher, were not for him.

As a young man, he had received an unmistakable call into ministry. But when Mordecai finished school, he went to work as a salesman.

God never gives up on us, though, even when we give up on Him.

About the time Mordecai became comfortable in his new life as a struggling salesman. God knocked on his door to remind him of His calling. It just may not have been in the way you might think – God does work in mysterious ways.

His grandpa Ham died. This grandfather had been a strong pillar of faith all of his life. He had always been there for Mordecai and everyone he knew. Grandpa Ham could preach to a young child and make him or her fall in love with Jesus. He could get an alcoholic, that held tight to the bottle – daily, and get them to walk away from it with Christ in his heart. He counseled young married couples struggling to make their marriage work, leaving them with renewed hope for their future. Grandpa Ham was a man of God, unlike any he had ever known.

When Mordecai received word that his grandpa had died, he knew exactly what he must do. He left his job of being a salesman not to just preach, but to become a traveling evangelist.

When he began, he often preached for free. When they passed the offering plate, the money was barely enough to keep him going. However, God always made a way for him to get to the next town, to preach the next message.

As an evangelist, he realized he would sometimes say things that people didn't want to hear. Several times he was attacked and almost killed, but that didn't stop this man of God. He kept preaching, refusing to be silenced out of fear or defeat.

But as he continued to share the Word of God, lives began to change. As he traveled to the next town, the crowds grew. Sometimes a two-night revival meeting would extend for an entire week, due to the demand and lives being changed. Mordecai only left due to his commitment in the next town.

One day, he was preaching at a tent revival meeting in Charlotte, North Carolina. He began with these words, "There's a great sinner in this place tonight."

Can you imagine hearing that in a church today? I mean, I think most people would just exit immediately with that opening.

But the young Billy Graham and his friend Grady Wilson were there that night. They had taken refuge in the church choir behind the pulpit so that they didn't have to face Evangelist Ham.

Even though they were afraid of his wrath and fiery preaching, they were drawn to the revival where thousands of people were gathering every night. They'd heard stories of lives being changed.

As a teen, Billy's life was all about baseball. He was far away from God and admitted he had no interest in church. But that night, everything changed. God did a powerful work in his heart, and both Billy Graham and his friend Grady were saved. The rest is history. (McDaniel, 2018).

But the lesson for us might not necessarily be about Billy Graham. Perhaps it is about a man from Kentucky whose family was so poor that food was often not available. Yet, his life mattered in a way that is beyond calculation.

Did he set out to bring the next great evangelist to Christ in that tent revival meeting in Charlotte? Of course not, He set out to do what he was called to do and speak the words that needed to be said, without worrying about whether they would be successful or not. He was there to do a job and left the success up to the One who called him—God Almighty. His faithfulness to that calling changed the world.

~

Sometimes we may wonder if what we do matters, especially when we see how fragile life can be. The loss of a loved one can make us want to quit. But what if, like Mordecai, we turn it around and the worst becomes the motivation for the best that is to come?

There are so many stories I could share here. When I lost my wife and daughter in 2000, I was very certain that I was done. My life was over. I didn't want to live. I couldn't see beyond the pain.

But only by God am I here today. I'm not saying that it's easy. I am saying that it is not over. If you will lean into God Almighty, His grace and strength will see you through and He will open doors for you that you never knew even existed.

Warrick Dunn

When we look at those who seem to have to all, often we think that their lives are so easy and that they seem to get all the breaks. I mean, when we look at an NFL star, for instance, we think, "What a life."

What about their back story? There was one young man who grew up in Baton Rouge, Louisiana. He was raised by a single mom, with four other siblings. She instilled in her children that if you work hard, you can make something of yourself.

She led by example. She worked as a police officer, and also took extra jobs, like off-duty security, to help make ends meet. She loved all her children, but the oldest was the leader, in school, on the football field, in track, and in everything he did.

His mom loved to go watch this young man work his magic on the field. He could do everything. Offense, defense, quarterback, running back, cornerback and receiver. He never got off the field and he loved it that way. So did she. He was going to go to college with his gifts and she was so proud.

Then one evening, while she was working an off-duty security job escorting a business owner to make a late-night deposit at the bank, the unthinkable happened. She was killed by two armed robbers.

Two days after Warrick, the oldest son celebrated his eighteenth birthday, he went from football star, to head of a household of six. What was he to do? Forego his scholarship opportunity and stay home and take care of the kids?

He figured out a way to do both. His unlikely story became historic. He not only played football at the highest college level, but he also went on to have a storied NFL career.

That is only part of the story though. He created a program that helped single mothers achieve homeownership and helped countless families along the way. He believed that was one way of giving back what his mother had given him.

Despite all of his achievements, he still struggled with the grief of that horrific loss and would sink into depression regularly. He buried himself in his work and charitable causes as a form of self-medication, to block out the pain. But the suffering continued.

Then one day he decided, after years of counseling, to confront his mom's killers. He had been hanging on to that pain, hatred, and unforgiveness too long. So calls were made and times were set and then rescheduled. The day finally came for him to meet his mother's killers. Only one of them came to the visitation room. No reason was ever given for the one who wouldn't come. But the one who did show up (Kevan Brumfield), was the man who had confessed to the killing that fateful night.

The drive to Angola State Prison is a long one. The drive back to death row, even longer. When the meeting took place, Brumfield's attorneys told Warrick that he would answer no questions about the night because of pending appeals. While

Warrick was unsure what to do, he knew he had to face this man, and he had to do it now.

The meeting was not what he expected and it changed his life. He was able to forgive what most would deem unforgivable. He talked with the man for an hour about life on the streets and the impact that the loss of his mom had on the family. Brumfield told Warrick that he had followed his career and knew that he was nearing Hall of Fame numbers. He shared that he was not that man he use to be anymore and that if he had not been locked up, he would probably be dead by now. He also told Warrick that he had been praying for him and his family. He told Warrick, "I always felt that you were an amazing person. Today proved it. Just live life man." (Dunn, 2008)

While Warrick was never locked up, this set him free. He had been afraid to get involved in relationships because of the potential loss. Until then, he had been robbed of the emotions of joy and happiness. Pain, anger, and hatred had been fueling a fire in this man and had almost consumed his life.

Sometimes, we need to forgive to live. That's what Warrick Dunn did that day at Angola State Prison in Louisiana, and it made all the difference in the world to him.

We can't forget that our life does matter. It matters first to us, and if we are holding on to something from the past, it becomes like a weight around our neck that wants to drown us. When we hold onto the pain of abuse or neglect or worse, it may fuel us for a while. However, eventually, it kills our soul and holds us hostage in a prison cell of our making.

We might not realize it, but we are the only ones with the keys to open the cell. Once we do, our lives become more than we could ever imagine.

Warrick Dunn went on to do more for other people and has joined causes that have multiplied his efforts. He excelled in football, rushing for over 10,000 yards, a feat only a few running backs in history have done.

So, I'm speaking directly to you.

> *"Have you allowed your past to dictate your future,*
> *holding you back from the greatness inside of you?*
> *Are you holding onto hatred and anger*
> *that is killing you?"*

Maybe it is time to let it go and forgive. Not for the person who hurt you, but for you. It will set you free. Your life matters way too much to allow it to be squelched by the past.

Let it go.

Rise above it.

I need you to hear that I have seen the good of the Lord, in the land of the living.

I have also seen great tragedy in life.

I have seen God use the very worst events in my life to bring about amazing things when I surrendered my pain to Him.

I am convinced that God will do the same for you.

The more years that pass by, the more I realize life is short. Maybe you've discovered that too. I desire nothing else than to make every bit of time count, like this book that I am writing and you are reading. I believe that this time matters for a purpose far greater than I can fathom. God has a purpose for this time and I hope I am faithful in it.

Life may not always go like I think it should, but God is faithful. His word says that He will give us favor and blessing to do all that He's asked us to do.

We may never see the full fruits in our lifetime. But it doesn't mean it's not making a difference. We can trust that the good work that we are doing is changing the world. So, when you are wondering about your value and whether your life matters or not, let these stories resonate in your soul.

Chapter 7
PTSD

Men and women have been going to war in various parts of the world since the beginning of time. Each time they do, they leave a part of themselves—if not all of themselves—there, on the battlefield. Often the battlefield comes home with them.

War forever changes a person. Each person is affected in his or her own way. The impact on soldiers is so diverse that it has baffled everyone who has tried to come up with some formulaic way of addressing it. How do you help a person assimilate back into a world where people aren't shooting at them or planting improvised explosive devices (IEDs) meant to blow them to kingdom come?

We can trace PTSD in some form or another back to the Greco-Persian wars. Wherever mankind goes to war, some scars are seen. Others remain hidden. Where there are scars, there is pain. And where there is pain there is a need for healing. Too often, when it comes to our internal scars, they go untouched, unshared, and certainly unhealed

American soldiers first experienced post-traumatic stress disorder (PTSD) in the Revolutionary War against England. Only after significant advances in military technology did the problem show up in large numbers. That happened during the Civil War, where PTSD was called by a variety of names, like – "acute mania", nostalgia (now known to have been depression), or a condition called – "soldiers heart" (which was most likely high anxiety due to the invisible scars of war on the mind). In World War I, due to the nature of trench warfare, constant shelling, and the use of "mustard gas", led to terms such as "shell shock" and "gas hysteria" being used to describe soldiers' symptoms (Horowitz, 2015).

While there have been many terms for PTSD over the years, how it is to be treated, or whether it can be treated, has remained a moving target. It has led many that suffer from it, to end their own lives.

.According to research in this field, almost 70% of veterans who suffer from PTSD do not know that there are methods to help heal. And of those that know that there are treatment options, many do not always trust them.

PTSD's partner, depression, adds to the challenge. The Veterans Administration (VA) statistics tell us that someone is 300% more likely to suffer from depression if they have PTSD.

This shocking number goes hand in hand with the statistics that show that those with PTSD are far more likely to commit suicide. Yet, when depression is added to the mix, it skyrockets the numbers dramatically. Visit the VA website or the NIH for current statistics.

My experience working with those that have PTSD has not been confined to those in the military alone. I have counseled women who have suffered from sexual trauma and betrayal trauma that create the same results. What is also interesting is that one of the fastest-growing groups that suffer from PTSD is adolescents. Visit the National Institute for Mental Health website for current statistics.

One story about a command driver in Iraq during the post-Desert Storm—Operation Enduring Freedom resounds deeply in my soul. A young man joined the Army, right out of high school in South Texas. He was a tough kid that grew up outdoors in the hot South Texas sun. He was a high school athlete, a preacher's kid, and a man of faith. Not ready to go to college after high school, he always wanted to join the Army, like many in his family had done. He was determined to follow in his father's footsteps, who had served in Vietnam.

Because he was in good physical condition, he breezed through basic training, though many found it difficult. He excelled at the physical challenges and wanted more. He shot a rifle well and handled other weapons with just as much ease.

When he went to Advanced Infantry Training, he excelled there as well. It seemed he could do everything they asked of him.

After he completed his training and was assigned to a unit, he asked for Airborne training. He qualified, but the current classes were filled. He would have to wait for the next available slot.

His unit deployed to Iraq. There, he drove an armored personnel carrier. He saw a lot of action from the day he arrived. There were mortar rounds lobbed at his unit as they were departing the airfield. When they took cover, snipers fired at them. They all survived the first day, but it was a rough introduction to war and Iraq.

As they patrolled, the mine sensing gear on the vehicle in front of the convoy picked up on what might be an improvised explosive device (IED). When the bomb techs got out to investigate the IED detonated.

The enemy had waited in the distance and triggered it. They must have been a bit anxious because no one was close enough yet for any damage to occur. They had set it off too early. But the explosion rocked the convoy and our young driver was rocked a bit as well.

It was one thing to see the enemy and engage them with your rifle or artillery. But it was another to have booby-traps and remote detonation IEDs going off with no warning. He was not prepared for this, nor was anyone, but he soldiered on.

Over the next months of convoys, the group confronted the enemy almost daily and did their job well. Then came the day that no one saw coming. The mine-sensing vehicle stopped, signaling that there was a problem. Feeling like he was in a dream, the explosion went off right under their vehicle. It came with such force that the command vehicle was flipped upside down. Outside it rained liquid metal and a pink mist.

Once our young driver regained consciousness, he could only see smoke. He felt blood coming down his face. Other vehicles in his convoy were engaging the enemy. He could hear the gunfire and the tanks booming away.

Members of his unit came and began cutting the doors off of the armored personnel carrier to get them out. One person in the command vehicle was dead, and all of the others were wounded but survived.

When our young driver emerged and could finally clear his eyes, he saw a medic looking him over. He asked the medic what happened.

The medic told him that the bomb-sensing vehicle had missed the bomb that was right underneath them. When they stopped, it was remotely detonated.

The young man asked, where was the vehicle and what happened to the soldiers?

The medic just shook his head. "They're gone … there is almost nothing left. You guys are lucky to be alive. If that vehicle had been four or five feet farther up the road, the blast would have incinerated your vehicle too."

The young man began to doubt whether he could do this anymore. But, like a good soldier, he carried on, tucking away those feeling and images in his mind, hoping to forget.

Each time they went out, it became harder and harder. It wasn't because the enemy was that much worse, but the enemy was in his head. He couldn't forget one of his good friends from basic training had been in the vehicle that was lost. They had just had a conversation that morning, right before the convoy headed out.

His friend told him, "Don't worry big guy, we are taking the lead and we won't let anything get to you guys." He gave his life to keep his word.

As time passed, they caught random gunfire, an occasional rocket or mortar fire, but our young driver just kept on. He was a good soldier and was determined to do his best. He defended this unit the best he knew how to do. He fired his rifle when needed. He drove as he was trained and the conditions dictated. He did his job. Each time, he tucked away the next loss, close call, explosion, or look in the enemy's eyes when his rifle shot met its mark.

When it was time to load up and ship out, our young man wasn't sure what to expect but he was looking forward to the break. He slept most of the way back home on the Air Force C-141.

When he arrived in the United States, he was able to go home on leave. His parents met him at the airport in Houston and gave him a hero's welcome. People in the airport terminal cheered our young man as he walked with his family.

Just before he stepped out of the terminal, he saw an Arab man look up from his phone after pushing a button on it, looking right at him. Our young soldier had seen this before in Iraq and it was often a signal that something bad was about to happen. He froze in place. His family walked a few more steps, but his father noticed and went back for him.

"What's wrong, son?" His father asked.

"I just saw something that … oh it was nothing. Sorry. It is just a major adjustment being back in the normal world." Our young man said. He tucked this feeling away too, but with a heightened sense of awareness that around any corner there could be an enemy waiting to exploit their weakness.

On the way home, he tried to engage with his family but struggled. He was constantly scanning the other vehicles looking for threats, looking for signs of roadside disturbances that might signal an IED placement.

He thought he must be going crazy. In his mind, he could see threats everywhere and everyone was oblivious. So, he swallowed his fear and put on a brave face, and did his best to engage with his loving family.

When he got to the family home, the church had set out a big welcome home meal. Everyone hugged him and shook his hand. Some of the old men shared war stories of their own. They would ask him for stories, but he just said, "nothing much to tell. It is tough and the enemy is serious."

That would be all. And yet, each time, in his mind, the events would all play out in living color and sound, as if they were happening again. He thought no one would understand, so he kept it all to himself.

When the crowd of well-wishers finally left, he told his family he was tired and wanted to shower and go to sleep. They helped carry his belongings to his room. His Mom and Dad hugged him, his older brother slugged him in the shoulder and told him that he was proud of him. His sister kissed him on the cheek. He smiled and thanked them all.

In the shower, he hoped the sand from the desert was going to finally be washed away. But it didn't, no matter how hard he scrubbed. More than sand needed to be washed away.

When he finally laid down and closed his eyes, he was immediately asleep, but that's when the dreams played in his head.

The tracer rounds went out and came in. The ground shook from an explosion. Someone's voice came over the radio, then went silent in mid-sentence. That could only mean one thing.

The vehicle he had been driving lifted up and rolled over, leaving his body hanging upside down from a seatbelt, with blood dripping down his face. Every detail replayed in his dreams as if he were still there.

He couldn't tell his family what was going on. He wasn't okay but didn't want to burden them with something they wouldn't understand.

And yet, they could see that something wasn't right—they knew him well enough to know what no sleep looked like.

He brushed their concerns to the side.

One afternoon, a West Texas wind whipped across the house, slamming the door so hard the house rattled. He immediately hit the floor and covered his head.

When he lifted his head, everyone in the house stood staring at him with mouths wide open. No mortar round. Just wind. He shook his head, got to his feet, and fumbled an apology. Before anyone could speak to him, he hurried to his room.

Behind the closed door of his room, he threw himself on his bed and began to weep. He wept from the deepest pit of his soul over the things he had seen, the people he had lost, and the people that he had killed. Every image and face came rushing back to his mind and he didn't know what to do to make it stop.

Then he remembered his old Master Sargent, who had served at the end of Vietnam. He drank a lot and wouldn't talk about his experiences over there. He guessed he was drowning the demons he saw that must be like his own. The stories of guys getting into drugs didn't make sense, until now. That must have been how they stopped the never-ending replay of the memories from hell.

Some had taken their own lives. He now understood that level of desperation. He also knew he was headed down the same path. He knew he had to walk out of that room and get some help from his family and any means necessary, or he would end up like them.

He dropped to his knees and prayed. God must have an answer for him. During his prayer, his father came in, and with tears in the old pastor's eyes, he knelt beside his son, wrapping his arms around him.

Together, they prayed for what seemed like hours. The young man spoke to God about the things that he had seen, experienced, and done—all of it. He asked God to forgive him where he had failed. He wasn't sure where he had failed but it sure felt like he had. He asked God to take away the dreams and the fear of living with this burden. To help him lay it down at the foot of the cross. To help those families that had been struck by this war in all the different ways that war can destroy lives. He prayed for the courage to finish his tour of duty and then walk away into a new life. He prayed for the help he would need to recover mentally and the strength to stay away from those things that could impair his mind, like drugs or alcohol.

He felt God's presence. A simple phrase came to his heart, that could have only come from God. "I will."

He got up from the floor, helping his father, who swore he didn't need the help. They walked into the family room where everyone was talking quietly. He sat down next to his sister. Looking around the room, he finally smiled.

He took his sister's hand and told the family, "I need to tell you guys the stories of what happened while I was in Iraq. The things I have seen, done, and lived through are pretty rough, but I know that if I do not get them out now, I never will."

And so in the very comfortable living room, he talked while they listened. Now and then, someone asked a question where they wanted to know more.

His Mom left the room briefly to order pizza and get something for everyone to drink. She would have rather cooked but didn't want to miss a thing.

When the pizza arrived, they ate and continued the conversation until long after midnight. Some shed tears. Some had exclamations of shock. When he finished, silence filled the room, along with a new sense of overwhelming respect for their son/brother/soldier.

The young man felt like the weight of the world had been lifted from his shoulders. When he went to bed that night, he was finally able to sleep, really sleep.

When he got up the next day, he had renewed sense of purpose and knew that he needed to make sure that he kept talking about it and that he needed to see a professional counselor. He would not allow anyone's opinion about getting help to deter him.

He was scheduled to fly back to his base the next day and wanted to spend all this time with his family. The guys got together and played a round of golf.

The ladies planned a going-away party for the young man. It was wonderful. They invited all of his old friends that were close enough to come and when they got home after their golf game, he was overwhelmed with the love of his family and friends again.

But this time was different. They knew him, and they had also heard from him - all that he had been through, leaving nothing out. Knowing they knew all he had been through, and that they loved him, made all the difference in the world.

When he returned to his base, he sought out counseling. In the remaining year of his enlistment, he went to college on the base in between his work details.

When they asked if he wanted to reenlist—and they made the offer very attractive—he respectfully declined. He planned to finish that degree and have a family. And that is exactly what he did. He is now the husband of a beautiful woman and the father of a houseful of wonderful kids. He works at a great job for a big company.

He also still sees a counselor a couple of times a year, just to stay proactive. It helps. And, he now helps other veterans who are dealing with PTSD as a peer-support specialist volunteer. He says that helps him as much as anyone.

This young man's life matters! He is an American Hero, that served our country. He continues to serve others in both small and large ways, the best that he can. At each point in his life, he was making an impact on those around him. I wonder how many lives his service in the military impacted? I wonder how many lives he saved through his valor? In turn, how many families, kids, co-workers, employers, churches, or others did his life intersect with, either directly or indirectly, in a positive way?

Even if it was just one – his life would matter. Does this story resonate with you? If you are someone who experiences PTSD, I want you to know that there is help. Reach out to www.thewarriorsrefuge.us and ask for counseling. We will either provide counseling or we will find you a counselor close to where you are. You are not alone and help is available!

YOUR LIFE MATTERS!

Dr. Cliff Robertson, Jr.

Chapter 8
Suicide

I am deeply concerned that the suicide rate in this country is astronomical. Veterans are dying at a rate of twenty-two every day, almost one an hour, due to suicide.

According to the National Institute of Mental Health, in 2019 almost six people per hour died of suicide in America. The majority of those were between the ages of twenty-five and forty-four. I believe that this reflects a sense of hopelessness in our world that has become systemic and deadly.

But why has it become this way?

While there is no consensus among the experts, it is my opinion that it has a lot to do with self-image and the way we perceive ourselves in the world. I believe that if everyone truly believed that their lives mattered, they could overcome anything that life throws their way.

We can read in the Bible, "In this life, you will have tribulation." (John 16:33) In other words, bad things are going to happen, even to good people. No one escapes unscathed by the ravages of time. But how do we face these challenges? How do we overcome them? Why do we allow them to overwhelm us and lead us down a path to our self-demise?

Perhaps we could ask this,

"Who do we allow to speak into our lives?"

Whoever we give that permission to, also has a certain amount of control over us. When we sacrifice that control by giving it to someone else, aren't we abdicating our responsibility for our mental health and well-being?

In essence, we're saying that person knows more about us than we do and we should let them control how we think about ourselves. Maybe that's part of how we get off track and start to lose our way.

Sometimes it isn't someone trying to manipulate us. Sometimes it's simply someone or some organization doing their job that we allow it to control or overwhelm us.

For example, when I lived in eastern Texas, there was this great guy that we will call James. He was a kind older man, who had retired and had a big family. One day James fell and broke his leg. Being an older man, it took a while for his fractured leg to heal. After some time in an inpatient rehabilitation facility, they sent him home for in-home rehab, as well. Gradually, he was able to walk with a cane and he seemed to be in good spirits.

When the hospital and doctor bills came in, he read the totals and realized that he didn't have that kind of money. He went to the bank to try to borrow enough to cover his bill.

The banker looked at him quizzically and shook his head. "No. The insurance will surely pay for most of this. After they do, whatever is left, we will see what we can do to help."

Once James heard the word "No," he heard nothing after that. He believed he was responsible for the whole bill and insurance had either not covered it or had already paid all that they were going to pay.

So he decided to sell his belongings. He asked someone to help get his car fixed up so he could sell it, and maybe get part of their land cleared and fenced off so he could sell that, too.

His son was stupefied by his father's behavior. So, he asked him, "Why are you suddenly wanting to sell these things? Is there a problem?"

James told his son that the bills were due and that he had no other way to pay them. He had to take drastic action or they would come and throw him in jail and take everything.

His son explained that he had insurance to help with the bills and that these statements were customary. "Just chill, Dad. It's going to be okay."

The father screamed at his son, "If they are not due for me to pay, they would have never been sent to me to pay, with due dates in the next week! Some even due immediately!" James broke down and cried.

The son comforted his father the best he could, but he remained baffled at his reaction.

James told him, "If I can't find a way to sell some of this stuff and pay them, then I will die before I let them take everything I have ever worked for. I must be worth more dead than alive."

These words broke his son's heart, but nothing that he said to his father changed his mind. So, he called their pastor, a man his father respected very much. When he explained the situation, the pastor cleared his schedule and opened his office doors for them as soon as they could get there.

When they arrived, the pastor came out from behind his desk and gave James a hearty handshake and brotherly hug.

James talked about the bills and how he didn't have the money to pay.

The pastor asked him about insurance.

James told him what he believed to be true, that his insurance had paid all they were going to. Either that or that his clumsy fall was not covered. He didn't know which, but he did know that he didn't have the money.

The pastor explained, "This is common. You, James, being a good and honorable man, who always pays his bills would normally worry about such things. But insurance companies get the bills for your medical work at the same time that you do. They're required to send them to you so that if there are any discrepancies, you will see them and question them. Give it a month or so and you will see the insurance response to the bills and trust me when I say, this is going to be just fine. God has you right in the palm of His hand and He will take care of you, just as He always has."

They prayed and everything seemed to be okay. The son took his father home. They sat and talked a little while over a cup of coffee.

James seemed to be better and didn't want his son to worry about him anymore. So, he ushered his son off because he had taken the day off from work to help. He didn't want to be a burden to anyone.

The son told him, "Dad, you are no burden. I am here for you and Mom. Always."

James told his son, "Let's not worry Mom over this, okay?"

He replied, "Yes, Dad," and returned to work, leaving his dad in what seemed to be better spirits.

After his son left, James went back to his desk and calculated the totals again. He phoned the insurance company, but they put him on hold for what seemed like an eternity.

When someone finally picked up, they told him that the bills were in review and that if they reject the claim, he would be responsible for the debt in full.

He asked, "what's the likelihood of that happening?"

The insurance company representative told him that he had no way of knowing until the claim was reviewed and examined. It could take a while to sort out.

James inquired, "All of these bills say, 'Due Upon Receipt'. What am I supposed to do about it while you guys are reviewing them?"

The insurance guy answered, "You could always pay it. Then if we approve the claim, we would reimburse you. But that could take a long time."

James became despondent, worried that bill collectors would come and take everything he owned. He remembered something and ruffled through his papers, looking for it. He dug until he finally had it in his hand.

Reading the document, he breathed a ragged sigh of relief, sort of. He called the company that had issued the policy. They affirmed that it was in force and he was in good standing. In the event of his death, it would pay his surviving beneficiary the value of the policy.

He set down the phone and planned the only viable solution he knew.

His wife had come home from visiting with her friends and busied herself preparing dinner.

James went in to check on her and told her that it smelled great. He looked forward to her fine cooking. Then, he went into the gun cabinet in the living room and grabbed the shotgun, along with a couple of shells. He took them out the front door to his truck. He laid them on the seat and then locked the door. He was settled. This was the answer.

When he went back inside the house, the aroma of the wonderful meal his wife cooked filled their home. He sat down at the table with her and they enjoyed their meal.

She told him about her day and visiting with her friends, but noticed something was wrong with James. "How are you feeling today?"

He said, "I am hurting a little bit today. I also got all of those bills in from the hospitals and doctors. But it is all going to be okay."

She thought there was something more that he wasn't saying but, she decided not to push. The pain associated with his healing was probably why he felt bad.

After dinner, he helped her with the dishes but she quickly ran him out of the kitchen, telling him that he needed to prop up his leg, if it was ever going to heal.

He followed her instructions and went into the living room. He had the remote control to the TV in his hand but didn't turn the TV on. He couldn't stop the thoughts of all the bills he owed. He considered the conversation from his pastor who had said that honorable men worried about such things. He thought about how the insurance company said that if they denied the claim that he would liable for all of it. He also remembered that the other insurance company said that if he passed, what his beneficiary would receive.

His wife walked toward the living room, so he clicked on the TV and found the local news channel, his normal routine.

She greeted him with a kiss on top of the head and told him that she was going to the bedroom to change and that she would be back shortly.

He couldn't pay attention to the TV. He tried to pray but he couldn't. He felt like the world was closing in around him and he could only see this very dark tunnel that was getting smaller and smaller.

His adoring wife came back and plopped down on the couch next to him. When he winced, she apologized and kissed him again.

He forced a smile to keep up a pretense on the outside, but inside he told himself he would miss her and her kisses. He didn't want her to lose everything. He believed he had reached the only solution.

After the news and the Johnny Carson Show, they went to bed. He couldn't sleep, so he stared at the ceiling. When her steady breathing indicated she was fast asleep, he slipped out of bed, put on his clothes. He wrote her a note and placed it on top of the policy saying, "I love you, I didn't know any other way. This should take care of everything."

He cranked his truck but didn't turn on the lights, afraid it might wake her up. He backed down the driveway, pulled out onto the dark blacktop, and accelerated off into the night, turning on his lights only after he cleared the house.

The next morning, the woman, turned over in bed when she heard a knock at her door. She noticed her husband wasn't beside her, but put on a robe and hurried to the door, passing her husband's desk.

She opened the door to find the local county sheriff, whom she knew, and one of his deputies.

The sheriff took off his wide-brimmed hat and told her, "Ma'am, we go back a long way. This has to be the most difficult visit I have ever had to make. But we found your husband this morning."

The woman collapsed and didn't hear anything else the sheriff had to say. Her world spun and sobs poured out of her, with an unstoppable force.

The young deputy had come upon the grisly scene that morning. He immediately ran the plates on the truck to see who it belonged to and then called his sheriff, who was still in bed. He asked dispatch to send an ambulance, but there was no point. He requested the coroner instead.

When the sheriff arrived, he recognized him immediately. Choking back tears of his own, he had known this man his entire life. He wanted to think that maybe there had been a robbery or some sort of foul play but a quick scan of the scene revealed that this was most certainly a suicide.

The sheriff stayed with the deceased's wife until the other family members arrived. After a little while, he handed his card to the man's son and said that he would like to talk with him sometime soon. The son walked out with the sheriff and replayed the conversations with his father over the past couple of days and his mental state. He relayed the conversation they had with the pastor and how everything seemed to be okay after that.

The son walked back into the house as the sheriff drove off and for some reason, went into his father's study area. He sat down, hoping to find a quiet place to sort through what had just happened. At first, he looked out the window, seeing the landscape, but not seeing anything.

He looked down at his own trembling hands and placed them on the desk to steady them. It seemed to help. Then he saw his father's handwriting on a note. It wasn't folded over to conceal, it was just lying there, on top of a stack of papers, but it was intended for his mom.

He carried it with as delicate a touch as possible to her and sat down next to her. He handed her the note. "I just found this in the study, on the desk."

She held the note a little bit away from her, to avoid staining it with the tears that dripped from her face. As she read it, she looked up at her son. "What is he talking about?"

He then handed her the life insurance policy the note was sitting on and told her about the conversations he had with his father and the pastor the day before.

She nodded, remembering how her husband had mentioned the bills and how she had dismissed his concerns, so lightly. Devastated, she sobbed again, with pain and moaning that was otherworldly. She believed she was at fault and would have to live with it the rest of her life.

The son, seeing his mom in such a state, felt the same pain. Was he at fault for not staying with his father? Could he have stayed with him longer? Talked with him again? Called the insurance companies again? But he knew his father would have been too proud for that. Even though it was neither the fault of the son nor the wife, guilt rained down on them both, like acid burning their souls. Nothing they could do would make it better at that moment.

This is a tragic true story, but it happens to hundreds of families each week, thousands each year.

Someone once asked me, "what does it matter if I commit suicide?"

Imagine the impact it would have on the ones who love you or know you. We do not live in a bubble where our lives impact no one. The loss of our life hurts others. When it is from suicide, the ripple effect is horrific. The first waves, after a suicide, are close by, and big. "As they move outward, they get smaller and smaller. The reach of the pebble's waves is much greater than the size of the pebble itself.

"When someone dies by suicide, the people impacted most dramatically by those first waves are those closest to the person who died: family, friends, co-workers, classmates." (Sandler, 2018). Naturally, the people who interacted the most with them, will miss the physical presence of that person and typically feel the loss most closely. Often, the people most close to them feel they may have failed in some way. As the widow and son in the previous tragedy, they all must live with that guilt of wondering if they could have done more. The pain of that guilt is so horrible, some of those grieving take their lives because of it.

"But those people represent only the first wave or the initial level of impact. Members of an individual's community, such as members of a faith community; teachers, staff, and other students in a school; or service providers, may also be affected by a suicide. They will also grieve, wondering if they could have done more.

"People who may not have even personally known the individual who died can also be impacted. Emergency medical personnel, law enforcement, clergy, and others who respond and provide support to the family and community, either at the time of death or afterward can replay the scene and question if they made an error in their actions or timing." (Sandler, 2018).

Ultimately, like a pond is changed because of a single pebble, an entire community can be changed by a suicide. According to a 2016 NIH study on exposure to suicide, an estimated 115 people are exposed to any particular suicide, with one in five of those reporting that this experience had a devastating impact or caused a major-life disruption.

Sometimes, it takes a village or a refuge,

The suicide epidemic among veterans is devastating, but I want to share a story that I find pretty inspiring.

A veteran, Bob (name changed), returned home from a deployment in Iraq and Afghanistan. His life was rough. He didn't know how to operate, now that he wasn't a soldier any longer. He struggled with his current paradigm and how to even view the people who were trying to help him.

So he drank to drown the images and the thoughts that were destroying him. He found drugs to further numb himself in between drinking binges. When Bob had to appear in court, facing some time, he believed that his life was over.

After that court appearance, he purchased a gun. He bought ammunition from a different store. He then went to a liquor store to buy his final bottle of whiskey to drown his sorrows that would soon end.

Before driving out to a secluded locale to drink and end it all, he went into a convenience store to get a notepad to write down a few words for his family that would hopefully explain what he was about to do. He stood at the counter paying when a friend that he had served with came in and shouted his name, "Bob, how the hell are you doing?"

With a big grin on his face, he slapped Bob on the back and gave him a big bear hug, almost wrestling him to the ground, a friendly greeting they had used in the past. They talked a bit and then Jim, the friend, asked Bob, "Whatcha' got there? Note pad for your last will and testament?"

Jim meant it as a joke, but the despair on Bob's face told him he had hit the nail on the head. He walked Bob to his truck. There, Bob told him how he had lost everything, had no place to go anymore, and couldn't function in this world, and that he was done trying.

Jim put his hand on his friend's shoulder and said, "We're going to get you some help." Jim called another friend who worked for a veteran non-profit that provided shelter, counseling, and career training. A couple more phone calls later and they were on their way to The Warriors Refuge in West Columbia, Texas.

At first, it wasn't easy for Bob to realize he needed a place like The Refuge. Shouldn't a soldier know what to do to work the problem? His mind raced to find one good reason why he didn't need help, finally wondering if he was already beyond help.

Then Bob questioned, "What if this is exactly what I need?"

Before long, he was thriving again. After some counseling, he found a job that was perfect for him. He also started going to church and met a woman who seemed to be perfect.

By starting at rock bottom, he found his foundation and now his life felt right. He had hope and a purpose. He started building a future that eight or nine months before, he thought didn't exist.

When he reached the end of his time at The Refuge, he reflected on that day after his court appearance, when he had bought the gun and ammo. Then that providential meeting with his battle buddy, Jim.

He considered all the different ways that his story could have played out. Bob cried, thinking of all he would have missed, meeting his future wife, being able to baptize his son, who he had just reunited with. He would have missed this new life that seemed so perfect.

He would have also missed his own salvation. While he attended a church service there at The Refuge, Bob realized he needed Jesus. He prayed with the pastor and by faith received Jesus into his heart. That was Bob's "aha" moment when he saw the world in a different light and his life began to truly change.

He felt a strength inside him that hadn't been there before. His life had been given a second chance and he was not about to waste it.

Now, here is my question. Who made all of this happen? Was it Jim? Was it the organization and all the people there? Was it the pastor?

Answer. All of them! All these lives mattered and they all helped to save this one life.

Bob now has a new wife, a child on the way, and is turning his life around and helping others. His life was almost over. Now he realizes that His Life Matters, even though it was almost over.

No matter where your life is today, your life matters. Whether you sweep the floors or help a friend in a time of need, all of it matters.

Your life matters.

One more note from me to you. If you are considering suicide, I want you to

call the national suicide lifeline right now.

1 800-273-8255

It's available 24/7

and offers free confidential support.

Dr. Cliff Robertson, Jr.

Section Two

The Tool Kit

for Changing Your World

Dr. Cliff Robertson, Jr.

Chapter 9

The power of God in your life

The greatest resource we can ever have—as the stories you already read in previous chapters have testified—is faith in God Almighty and the saving power of His Son, Jesus Christ. When we receive Christ as our Savior, we also receive the Holy Spirit, our advocate, and strength. His Holy Spirit lives in us with gifts and wisdom.

There is no greater resource found than in Him. I have seen Him move mountains in my life, including moving me into new areas and through doors that I never knew about. The truth is, God will make a way, even when no way previously existed.

Let's begin with God.

Some who read this book may not believe in God. Know that I respect that. However, I still believe that these words may resonate with you at some level because they are true. And if we are going to allow the right words into our lives, I believe, beginning with the best words is important.

What does God say about You?

You are His Masterpiece. In Ephesians 2:10, Paul wrote, "For you are God's Masterpiece, created anew in Christ Jesus, for the good work He ordained for you from the beginning."

Think about that word—masterpiece. He didn't call you a mess or a mistake. He didn't call you by any derogatory label whatsoever. He didn't say that if you follow these rules and jump through these hoops, buy these certain clothes and get everything just perfect, then one day you might be a masterpiece. He said, "you are God's masterpiece."

A masterpiece is something special that takes time to create, holds a special place in heart of the artist/Creator, and makes an impact on humanity. Something I love about the rest of the passage is that it makes room for transformation.

The word for masterpiece used here in Greek—the language the New Testament was written in—is the word *Poema*, meaning God's masterpiece.

But I want you to know this doesn't preclude us from having bad things come our way. We often make mistakes, bad choices, etc. We will have tragedy come our way and then there will things like an illness or a loss that we cannot explain. Life can be hard. He told us that it would be. (John 16:33)

So, what do we do when it gets tough, and we need to push the reset button? I just have one word here. Jesus.

The passage mentioned earlier about tribulation ends with, "but be of good cheer, for I have overcome the world." We will talk about that more later.

Back in Ephesians 2:10, the passage closes out with the truth that you are a masterpiece on a mission you were built for. To me, that's inspiring. I remember when I first read that passage and began to understand it. I thought, "Wow! Really? Me? You must be talking about someone else."

He wasn't. And I want you to know that God is talking about you too.

I am not trying to push my faith on you. The real question is what are you going to allow to speak into your life? Is it life-affirming and true, or is life-destroying?

What I want you to get from this part is something simple. You are special.

There are things that only you can do.

You are a masterpiece.

Extraordinary.

A world changer.

Your life matters.

But to get to this place of grace, you have to believe.

Faith matters.

We all put our faith in something. Most things we put faith in fade away.

But what if you gave God your faith? What do you have to lose? Better yet, what do you have to gain?

When I surrendered to God, I can honestly tell you that things began to change in my life for the good. Since that moment, not only have I never regretted the decision, but I have also come to cherish it even more, as the point of the greatest transformation in my life.

I have grown over the years in my faith and begin most days with Him in prayer and meditation on His word. The life of faith in the grace of our Lord comes with so much peace and strength.

He never tells us that it will be easy and that we won't have troubles. But He does tell us that He will be with us through it all. In the end, we will be with Him through all eternity. Does it get better than that? I don't think so.

You can begin this journey of faith with a simple prayer like this;

Lord, I believe in you, even though I am not completely sure what all of that means. You sent your Son, Jesus Christ, to die for me, so that I may have forgiveness of sin and eternal life.

Lord, please forgive me of all of my sins. I surrender my heart to you. I receive your gift of grace. Help me to grow closer to you as I live my life for you.

Fill me with the Holy Spirit and teach me to pray. I long to talk with you more. Open up your Word, like a treasure chest, full of rare and precious gems, perfectly fitted for my heart. In Jesus' name, I pray, amen.

If you prayed that prayer in faith, you are now my brother or sister in the family of God. Know that you are loved, and your identity is found in Him, a child of the King.

Prayer

You may have just prayed the given prayer, or maybe you have prayed something like it before. Maybe you are still thinking about it. Either way, I want to talk to you about the power of prayer.

The power of prayer is beyond compare. When we pray and believe, we are calling on the greatest resource in the universe to come to our aid. So how do we pray?

Several years back, a little old man came up to me and gave me two verses from the Bible, 1 Chronicles 4:10 and Jeremiah 29:11. He told me that I should pray these verses over my life.

Honestly, I had never prayed that way. I did not know the Bible very well, so these verses only had a vague place in my mind. I had no idea what he meant by "Pray these verses over your life."

The first thing I did was to look them up. 1 Chronicles 4:10 (KJV) "And Jabez called on the God of Israel, saying, Oh that thou wouldest bless me indeed, and enlarge my coast, and that thine hand might be with me, and that thou wouldest keep *me* from evil, that it may not grieve me! And God granted him that which he requested."

I had no idea what all of that meant. I could see that Jabez was asking for a blessing, a bigger coast, God's hand to be upon Him and help with evil.

But here is what caught my attention, God said, yes. There had to be something more to this prayer. So, I looked deeper into the

113

context and the original language and found some very interesting things.

First, when you read verse 9, right before this one, you discover Jabez's name came from his mother having difficulty in childbirth. It would be like naming a child Twelve-hour Delivery or C-Section. Reminds me of the Johnny Cash song, *A Boy Named Sue.*

Jabez didn't have a great name, but the verse also says that he was more honorable than his brothers. Even though he didn't have a good name, he didn't let that hold him back. With my history, I could relate to that.

The prayer began with a request for a blessing. Not just any kind of blessing but a blessing "indeed." In Hebrew, that is like putting four exclamation marks after the word bless. In other words, Jabez asked for all the blessings that heaven had for him and his family.

He doesn't say, "bless me with money or fame." He left the character of the blessing to God, but He wanted all the blessings that God had for Him.

And God said, yes.

He then asked for an enlarged coast. I was lost here, so again, I looked for answers. The word coast has to do with property and territory lines. He wanted more property. He knew that more property would allow him to grow his family and be able to feed them with the crops or the herds of cattle or sheep. The bottom line is that this would allow him to be able to do more for his family.

And God said, yes.

The next part of the verse says, "and that thine hand would be with me." What exactly is he asking for? I could use my imagination, but I wanted to know, really know. As I studied the meaning here, it became apparent Jabez knew that without God's hand—His presence, strength, guidance, and protection—all the blessings and property in the world would mean nothing. He realized he needed God with him every step of the way or he would fail.

And God said, yes.

The final part of the prayer was that God would, "keep me from evil, that it might not grieve me." There are two ways to look at this request. First, he wanted to be kept from evil, perhaps temptations such as alcohol, getting involved with the wrong people, or even a sexual temptation.

Another perspective is to protect him from all the evil that might want to take what he has been given. Thieves and robbers. I believe that he meant both.

And God said, yes.

As I considered this prayer, to which God said yes, I wanted to apply it to my life. Here is what I came up with.

"Lord God Almighty, in the name of Jesus I come before Your throne. I ask that You would bless me, holding nothing back—unloading heaven with all the blessings You have for me and my family. I pray that You would expand my opportunity to serve Your Kingdom and my family. I pray that Your hand would be with me in all I do, for without You, I will fail. And Lord, I pray that You would keep me from all trouble and every temptation, and put the right people in my life. I ask that You grant this request of Your humble servant, just as You granted it for Jabez so many years ago, amen."

A book, *The Prayer of Jabez*, by Bruce Wilkinson, takes this prayer even further. I suggest you read it. It challenges the reader to pray this prayer every day and record how God moves in your life in accordance with your prayers.

In my own life, I have prayed this prayer off and on for a long-time and I will tell you that God is a man of His word and will do the amazing for you if you will just ask. I have seen it happen in my life.

The next passage is a little easier to dissect. Jeremiah 29:11 (NLT), "For I know the plans I have for you," says the LORD. "They are plans for good and not for disaster, to give you a future and a hope."

We're going to keep this one simple. The Lord has plans for you. Let that sink in for a minute. The One who created everything has plans for you. They are plans for good. That's pretty exciting.

God didn't use the word "good" very often, but He first used it in Scripture about His creation, and then later about His creation-level good plans for you. He goes on to say that these plans are to give you a future and hope. Well, it isn't a far reach to think that good plans equate to a good future.

But when the word "hope" is added at the end, I see something special. "Hope" in the Bible has a different meaning than it does in today's common language.

Today, we might say, "I hope that works out for you." Truth be told, we have no clue whether it will work or even if it is a good idea.

When God used the word "hope," it meant something completely different. God's hope is a confident expectation that He will do exactly what He said He would do.

When I first looked at how to pray this, I wasn't sure. I just read the verse back to God and said, "may it be so in my life." But then I knew that there was more, so here is what I came up with.

"Lord God Almighty, in the name of Jesus, I read in Your Word that You have good plans for me. That is exciting to me that the Creator of the Universe would think such of me.

"Then You go on to tell me that they are plans to give me a good future and that I can put my hope in Your plans. Lord, I ask that You would reveal Your plans to me, as I am ready to accept them.

"Lord, I pray You would prepare and equip me for these plans, that I may not fail. Lord, I pray that the path would be laid out before me—well-marked, so I don't miss a thing, nor do I get off track. And Lord, will You give me a glimpse of what that future may hold? In times when the road gets tough, that image will help me to keep going, amen."

God has answered that prayer without a doubt, several times in my life. Sometimes the words change but the basics of it have been the same for a while now. There is so much more here but I want to leave you with this, God will make a way for you, even when one doesn't currently exist.

God made you and therefore you matter.

#YourLifeMatters!

Chapter 10

Understanding the Psychology of it All

Because I have studied both theology and psychology, I find that the two often speak the same language, especially in the field of Positive Psychology. The commonly accepted definition of Positive psychology is: "Positive psychology is the scientific study of what makes life most worth living" (Peterson, 2008).

To push this brief description a bit further, positive psychology is a scientific approach to studying human thoughts, feelings, and behavior, with a focus on strengths instead of weaknesses, building the good in life instead of repairing the bad, and taking the lives of average people up to "great" instead of focusing solely on moving those who are struggling up to "normal" (Peterson, 2008).

In a nutshell, positive psychology focuses on the positive events and influences in life, including positive attitudes such as happiness, joy, inspiration, and love. (Peterson, 2008) Positive traits will include gratitude, resilience, and compassion.

As a field, positive psychology considers topics like character strengths, optimism, life satisfaction, happiness, wellbeing, gratitude, compassion (as well as self-compassion), self-esteem and self-confidence, hope, and elevation. (Peterson, 2008). By studying these topics, they learn how to help people flourish and live their best lives.

Martin Seligman is a researcher with a broad range of experience in psychology. If you had never heard of the positive psychology movement until now, you still might have heard his name at some point. Seligman's research in the sixties and seventies laid the foundation for the well-known psychological theory of "learned helplessness." (Peterson, 2008).

This theory, backed by decades of research, explains how humans and animals can learn to become helpless and feel they have lost control over what happens to them.

Seligman ties this fact with depression, noting that many people suffering from depression also feel helpless. "His work on the subject provided inspiration, ideas, and evidence to back up many treatments for depressive symptoms, as well as strategies for preventing depression.

"While this is impressive enough on its own, Seligman knew that he had more to offer the psychology community and the world at large—in particular, more work on the positive, the uplifting, and the inspiring. After making a name for himself with learned helplessness, he turned his attention to other traits, characteristics, and perspectives that could be learned." (Peterson, 2008).

The research they conducted ended up being the foundation for his extensive findings that led to programs that involved breakthroughs for more work with children and members of the military.

Up to this point in the history of psychology and psychological research, the focus had been on how bad things can be, mentally speaking. The driving force behind psychological research was to discover more about mental illness, abnormal psychology, how traumatic events impacted the brain, the why behind the suffering, and pain, people experience mentally, and emotionally. And there was no attention being given to what makes people happy or what causes them to thrive.

"In general, the greatest potential benefit of positive psychology is that it teaches us the power of shifting one's perspective." (Peterson, 2008).

Positive psychology teaches how to shift many of our everyday behaviors, with concrete ideas for improving our quality of life.

Many people overestimate the impact of money on their happiness. Money helps, but not as much as you might think. Actually, the pursuit of wealth can make you less happy, more stressed, and run anxiety through the roof. Spending money on experiences often provides a bigger boost to happiness than spending money on material possessions.

Gratitude is a big contributor to happiness in life, suggesting that the more we cultivate gratitude, the happier we will be. (Peterson, 2008). I have learned that when I begin my day with gratitude in the form of my journal time—writing a few things I am grateful for—it shifts my perspective from the troubles of the day to the potential for good. It is a game-changer, for sure.

Giving hugs or other acts of physical affection may give you a big boost in oxytocin, which may provide greater trust, empathy, and motivation, as well as a lift to your overall wellbeing. I have found that this practice not only impacts the person giving the hugs, but it also impacts the person being hugged - along with the people who witness it. It can become contagious. Before you know it, the mood of everyone around you has been elevated by hugs.

Happiness is contagious. Like I mentioned earlier about hugs and happiness, increased happiness—with or without hugs—is contagious as well. Those with happy friends and significant others are more likely to be happy in the future. (Peterson, 2008). We want to be around others who are happy for a reason. We are drawn to it.

This is the focus of many techniques, exercises, and even entire programs based on positive psychology because a relatively small change in one's perspective can lead to astounding shifts in wellbeing and quality of life. Injecting a bit more optimism and gratitude into your life is a simple action that can give you a radically more positive outlook on life.

Positive psychology teaches how to shift many of our everyday behaviors, with concrete ideas for improving our quality of life.

Many people overestimate the impact of <u>money</u> on their happiness. It does have some influence, but not nearly as much as we might think, so focusing less on attaining wealth will likely make you happier. Spending money on experiences often provides a bigger boost to happiness than spending money on material possessions.

Gratitude is a big contributor to happiness in life, suggesting that the more we cultivate gratitude, the happier we will be. I have learned that when I begin my day with gratitude in the form of my journal time—writing a few things I am grateful for—it shifts my perspective from the troubles of the day to the potential for good. It is a game-changer, for sure.

Giving hugs or other shows of physical affection may give you a big boost in oxytocin, which may provide greater trust, empathy, and motivation, as well as a lift to your overall wellbeing. I have found that this practice not only impacts the person giving the hugs, but it also impacts the person being hugged along with the people who witness it. It can become contagious. Before you know it, the mood of everyone around you has been elevated by hugs.

Those who intentionally cultivate a positive mood that matches their outward emotion benefit by more genuinely experiencing the positive mood. In other words, "putting on a happy face" won't necessarily make you feel happier but putting in a little bit of effort to be happy, likely will.

Happiness is contagious. Like I mentioned earlier about hugs and happiness, increased happiness—with or without hugs—is contagious as well. Those with happy friends and significant others are more likely to be happy in the future. We want to be around others who are happy for a reason. We are drawn to it.

When we do good for others, through simple <u>acts of kindness,</u> not only do we get a boost in our personal happiness, it often leads others to do the same. It's like when a person in front of us in a drive-through line pays for our meal and then we do the same for the person behind us. It feels good.

I already mentioned how doing something for other people impacted me. Remember the flowers at Wal Mart? We don't always realize the way those actions influence the people around us—like the Butterfly Effect. You make a difference. #YourLifeMatters.

<u>Volunteering</u> time to a cause you believe in improves your wellbeing and life satisfaction and may even reduce symptoms of depression.

<u>Spending money on other people</u> results in greater happiness for the giver. (Peterson, 2008).

Studies have found that positive emotions boost our job performance and positive emotions in the workplace are contagious.

One of the benefits of practicing a positive psychological outlook is success. Not only does success make us happier, feeling happy and experiencing positive emotions increases our chances of success. (Peterson, 2008).

However, don't assume that refusing to acknowledge negative emotions or moods will equal success. The experts in the field of positive psychology found that "forcing people who are not naturally optimists to 'just think positively' can do more harm than good. Unrealistic optimism is detrimental, along with intense pessimism." (Peterson, 2008).

So, how does it work if we are to think positively helps, without avoiding the negative? It can all seem confusing. I believe it comes down to an honest assessment of ourselves, looking at who we are while focusing on our strengths and doing more for others.

Well-known positive psychologist Roy F. Baumeister and colleagues through extensive research found "the satisfaction of one's wants and needs boost happiness but have virtually no impact on meaningfulness. Focusing on obtaining what you want will increase your happiness, but you may have to do more to get a deeper sense of meaning in your life. Happiness can be a self-focused endeavor, while meaningfulness is more of an outward-focused life." (Peterson, 2008).

This is one reason I asked you to consider all the people you have touched positively throughout your life and how that has impacted their lives and then find ways you might be able to turn and do more in that arena.

"Givers" experience more meaning, while "receivers" experience more happiness. Think of children at Christmas morning, opening the gift they wanted all year.

To find more meaning in your life, try discovering who you are and what are you meant to do. That's authenticity and it's worth the effort to dig into.

Find your best gifts and talents. Many people have little to no clue what that looks like for themselves, and their lives have slipped into a path of least resistance. They feel stuck.

If you want to know your mission in life, you need to take some time alone to dream a little. If you feel stuck, I recommend taking a couple of personality and vocational assessments (several are free) to help you with ideas.

What can I do today with this information?

Here are some key takeaways to get you started:

Exercise. You don't have to do a lot. Twenty to thirty minutes three to five times per week. You can go for a walk, bike ride, or some other form of exercise that works for you. This will elevate your sense of wellbeing and give you a sense of purpose.

Journaling. Specifically, journal your gratitude by writing three to five things each day for which you are genuinely grateful. This will remind you of the things in life that are truly important and help you focus on the good that is real in your world.

Meditation. I understand that when I tell people to do this, the first image that comes to mind is a monk in a robe doing a Gregorian chant. I am not talking about that. Nor am I talking about someone sitting in the lotus position with incense burning for hours. My personal practice is prayer, then reading a devotional while journaling about what it means to me. This helps bring focus to my life and helps to clear my head of all the junk that the world wants to fill it with. I choose to replace that junk with something inspiring, encouraging, and uplifting. I write out what it means to me to cement it in my mind and heart. I find that writing out what resonates with me cements it in my mind and heart.

I suggest you spend five to ten minutes doing that, too. That's a good beginning point. Let the process lead you to spend more time in devotion and journaling when it seems right.

Giving of Yourself. The key is to give to someone, or to a group who cannot repay you. The gift will make a profound impact on them. But the truth is that if this becomes part of your weekly activity, it will have a dramatically positive effect on you as well. Research indicates it is like getting a $50,000 a year raise when you were only making $25,000. That's life-changing.

You might have already noticed that positive psychology is more than just positive thinking. It requires positive action taking.

But if you will do the simple things that I mentioned above, I believe that you will see things begin to shift in your life in ways that you never thought possible.

Note: If you are battling depression, anxiety, or other mental health disorders, please see a mental health professional—whether a counselor or a psychiatrist. The strategies that I suggest in this chapter will help you but do not replace the need for a competent mental health professional.

If finances are an issue there are lots of non-profit organizations that can help with this as well. Do not allow money to stand in the way of your mental and emotional health.

Chapter 11

Self-esteem, self-worth, and social media—identifying the voices that speak into our lives

The voices that we allow to speak into our lives can be good or bad, helpful or destructive. While it may seem obvious that we would always select the good, the reality is that we do not.

Gandhi once said, "I will not allow someone to walk through my mind with their dirty feet." What happens when someone has dirty feet? They leave behind a mess. The "dirty feet" or mess can come from the person who is constantly negative or complains all the time and is never happy. Or it could be the person who tries to control or manipulate us. And it might be someone that leads us into things that are far darker and more destructive, such as drugs or worse. That is exactly what happens when we allow the wrong messaging and influences to enter our lives from the people around us. It can make our lives a mess.

Another input source that impacts us daily is advertising. Not all advertising is bad. Without it, we would miss some of the greatest things that this world has to offer. But it can also be destructive.

A statistic from the National Institute for Mental Health (NIMH) is particularly disturbing to me. The number two killer of people between the ages of ten and thirty-four is suicide.

I believe that the images and messages that come through advertising and social media contribute to this tragedy. The NIMH lists the age-adjusted suicide rate as up over 35% from 1999 to 2018. The rise of social media and the hand-held devices during that same time can't be a coincidence.

This is an epidemic that no one is talking about. It's pretty easy to equate that percentage to the advent of social media and the explosion of internet-based advertising.

So what does advertising say to us?

If we buy their products, we will be cool, attract the right people, and get the girl, or guy or job or house... and everything else we want.

I find it interesting that people want to sell us something that is supposed to define who we are and how we are to feel about ourselves. Shouldn't we be the ones deciding who we are and how we feel about ourselves? Are we supposed to think that a status symbol we purchase is somehow symbolic of our self-worth?

If we do not buy it, then we are somehow worth less than those who do buy it? I find this whole manner of thinking insulting and demeaning.

Advertisers spend a lot of money trying to determine the best ways to manipulate the psyche of the public to sell more products. The level of manipulation here is more than just product sales.

While selling is their goal, they do it by defining your world with their product in it to the point where you think you can't live without it.

If we allow their manipulation into our thoughts, it can destroy and distort our self-image or create an artificial self-image—airbrushed to an impossible fantasy.

For them to say that we are not enough without the product, sounds a lot like bullying, to me. But, if you believe you can't be enough without the product and you can't afford it, then what are you supposed to do? Suffer in silence? Go into a mountain of debt? Steal it? Kill for it? Sadly, the manipulation of thought has already led some people to do all those things.

I'm not the only one who sees it. Some organizations do nothing but study the impacts of advertising on the population. According to a writer from the Media Awareness Network said, "Marketers should be held responsible for 'systematically creating anxiety, promoting envy, and fostering feelings of inadequacy and insecurity to sell us their products."

The effects of this type of advertising could be devastating. According to the article, "Eighty percent of ten-year-old girls have dieted, and at any one time, 50% of American women are currently dieting." Ten-year-old girls, third and fourth graders, should not be worried about dieting or weight loss.

If 80% of ten-year-old girls were concerned about losing weight in 2011, can you imagine how bad the current numbers are? How many people will be suffering from low self-esteem if we continue these devastating advertisement schemes ten years from now?

Young females are not the only demographics targeted in advertisements. Many males are becoming insecure about their physical appearance as advertising and other media images raise the standard and idealize well-built men.

Researchers are concerned about how this impacts men and boys and have seen an alarming increase in obsessive weight training and the use of anabolic steroids and dietary supplements that promise bigger muscles or more stamina for lifting. (PBS.org). Young men, according to the NIMH, are three times more likely to commit suicide than girls, essentially, they are more successful at their attempts. This is tragic and heartbreaking.

PBS's lesson plan for students of all ages "Exploring Media Messages" tells us that some of the objectives of the lesson are "to give participants guidance in taking a stand against negative media images, to explore where each individual stands on the issues of advertising and self-image, and ultimately, to help students learn to believe in themselves and not compare themselves to anyone else." (PBS.org.).

"American pop culture seems to have the ability to make women anywhere and everywhere feel absolutely terrible," said Jean Kilbourne, during a speech entitled, "Slim Hopes/Still Killing Us Softly: Advertising, Gender, and Obsession with Thinness." In a speech at a college campus she shared, "My argument today is not just that the image makes us all feel bad and causes problems as we attempt to emulate it, but that it does even more damage than that," said Kilbourne. "It really inflicts a kind of cultural trauma, one that contributes to a sense of disconnection that many women and certainly some men feel and experience."

The media monsters of today's society are flooding us with images of what is and what is not considered beautiful. "Their goal is to control that narrative to sell more products. The first thing that advertisers do is surround us with ideal female beauty," said Kilbourne. She added, "Airbrushed images are now what many young girls and women have come to judge themselves by. We end up comparing ourselves to an image that is completely artificial, absolutely constructed, and has nothing to do with human beings."

In reality, most of the images we see, whether video or still, have been filtered, enhanced, and polished to a point where we wouldn't even recognize the person if we saw them in real life. This is where our young girls are getting their definition of beauty. Filters and apps are now preloaded and installed on mobile phones for us to "enhance" our pictures.

Kilbourne also pointed out that former supermodel, Cindy Crawford, was quoted as saying, "I wish I looked like Cindy Crawford." Kilbourne did acknowledge that there are stereotypes out there about men that can harm them but pointed out that they are not constantly, "criticized, scrutinized, and judged," as women are. "There are stereotypes that harm men, but they tend to be less personal and less related to the body," said Kilbourne.

There is no denying the impact media has on its audience, said Kilbourne. He reported that within three years after the arrival of TV, the number of teens at risk of having an eating disorder more than doubled.

"There's a lot of contempt for women who do not live up to the standard, which is all of us as we age," said Kilbourne. "The greatest contempt is for women who are considered to be the least bit overweight." Food is another pawn used by advertisers to make us feel bad about ourselves. "We are encouraged to hate our bodies and to feel disconnected and then we are offered food as the solution," said Kilbourne. "Ads often encourage very unhealthy attitudes towards food." Food is now being portrayed as a substitution for relationships.

One ad questioned, "Does quality time have to be spent with a person?" Let's redefine quality time with a "_____." (You fill in the blank.)

"These ads are often funny, and they can seem trivial but some research suggests that subliminal content in food advertising contributes to eating disorders by deeply confusing sex and hunger, and not just sex and hunger, but connection," said Kilbourne. "So, if food is sex, it's the good girls who don't eat. Its influence is quick, it's cumulative, and for the most part, it's subconscious," said Kilbourne.

"Eating disorders and the obsession with thinness is a major public health problem, and what will solve it is prevention," said Kilbourne.

I believe that it is going to take more than just prevention. It is going to take a revolution in our way of thinking about ourselves. We are going to have to stop allowing the input of advertising to impact our way of seeing ourselves. We must recognize that the advertiser wants more than we should be willing to give. The images the advertiser portrays are not real or attainable but rather, a caricature. I believe that when we change the way we view advertising and gain some healthy perspective about who we are and want to be, then I believe it loses its hold on and control over us.

I remember all the cigarette ads that portrayed smoking as cool and necessary to be part of the "in-crowd." The Marlboro Man was a rugged and handsome man who was so cool. Every young boy wanted to be like the Marlboro Man. What is not cool is that the image was a lie.

One of the Marlboro men was afraid of horses and needed to be lifted onto the horse with a rope. Four of them died from smoking-related illnesses including Wayne McLaren. He died at age fifty-one. Mr. McLaren spent the last days of his life doing anti-smoking campaigns. He was quoted in the LA Times as saying, "No one should have to live and die this way."

I have to wonder how many people died from watching these ads that encouraged them to smoke? I wonder how many kids began smoking behind their houses, schools, and alleyways because of the influence of such ads?

Are we willing to die for this? Are we willing to die for an image? While no one in their right mind would answer yes to that question, our actions say something very different.

We have to get wrapped around the idea that we are more important than anything a product could possibly add to our lives. If we give away our lives for an unattainable, mythical image portrayed by advertising, then what does that say about us?

I believe that says that we do not know our worth, nor understand our true value. I believe we can change that too. I believe that you can change the world in your own way. But first, you have to reclaim your life. You do that by controlling who and what speaks into your life. That includes shutting down the social media voice into your life as well!

Social Media

Social media has become our primary means of communication. Daily, we see people online who seem to have perfect lives, with no trouble in their relationships or work. We see people on perfect vacations and buying new cars or new homes. We then look at our own lives and wonder why we don't have those things. We feel like we are somehow less. We feel that we are failures because our lives do not look like what our "friends" lives look like on Facebook or Instagram.

I want you to know that I believe there are many redeeming qualities in social media. It keeps people connected in this fast-paced world. It helps people marshal help when it is needed. It gets the word out about good things to people who would have never heard about it. This book is advertised on social media. It's not all bad.

But the way social media is intentionally structured can lead to a dopamine addiction that is destructive in more ways than we can even begin to consider.

Let me ask you a question - How many times have you checked your phone since you have been reading this book?

Two or three times? More?

It does not offend me at all. But the truth is that you have probably checked it three or four times that much. I struggle with it too. Interestingly, the makers of the social media world designed it to be like that. The more we look, comment, and check, the more successful they become. Therefore, they are driven to make it addictive. It literally defines success for them.

One of the key people inside Facebook, Chamath Palihapitiya, who is the former Vice President of User Growth, told a group of students at a major university that when he looked back at what he helped to create, he felt tremendous guilt. He discussed how they exploited consumer behavior by creating short-term, dopamine-driven feedback loops. He even was quoted as saying that this is "destroying how society works, by turning us all into bonafide addicts."

What we don't realize is that our brains are using the same wiring in our social media addiction, as we would for a slot machine or even cocaine.

You might say, "Isn't that pretty harsh? I mean, cocaine? Really?"

I know it seems out there but bear with me a minute. Studies are revealing our addiction to social media is leading to increased levels of depression, poor sleep quality, and as we know, increased risk of car wrecks, injury, or even death. We need to put down our phones while we are driving, due to the potential for distraction, but it is more than that.

As a counselor, I have studied the brain, albeit, on a limited scale. We have neural pathways that work with the release of dopamine. Dopamine is released when something positive happens. This could be some good news, sex, exercise, a feel-good stimulus like a drug, or a positive social interaction. In its basic sense, the purpose seems to be to make us feel good and to move us to repeat that behavior.

When it is something good for us, repeating that behavior is a good thing. But when it is bad for us, the result is the same. It still gets repeated due to the dopamine release. I imagine you are wondering why a positive social interaction is a bad thing.

The challenge is that social media is built to manipulate you and monopolize and monetize your time for their cause. To keep you coming back again and again. When you don't see the things you want, like "likes," "views," or messages/comments, you get depressed. Would you believe Instagram has an algorithm that withholds "likes" for a period of time from your notifications and then releases them in a big burst?

Why would they do that?

They do that so that you will keep checking in. Every time you check your social media, you see the advertising someone purchased. Then when they finally release all the notifications in a big flourish it is like you have spun the wheels on a slot machine enough times and it finally hit the jackpot. The bells are ringing, the coins are falling into the tray, and the dopamine is flooding your brain, causing immense pleasure and driving you to keep going.

In the intervening times, you are mentally riding a social media-driven roller coaster of emotions that can wreck your life.

How does that make you feel? When you are not getting the response that you want, you feel depressed and worthless, like you don't matter. Why? Because someone's algorithm is controlling and manipulating you. It is almost as if we have become puppets on strings, pulled about by the great puppet masters of social media. And the truth is, it's killing us.

A University of Pennsylvania study examined how social media use causes fear of missing out ("FOMO"). The study used two groups. One group of participants limited their time on social media to thirty minutes a day. Another group, acted as a control group, using Facebook, Snapchat, and Instagram as usual. The researchers tracked the participants' social media time automatically via iPhone battery usage screenshots.

The participants completed surveys about their mood and well-being. After three weeks, the participants who limited social media said that they felt less depressed and lonely than people who had no social media limits.

Psychologist Melissa Hunt, who led the study, explained, "Using less social media than you normally would, leads to significant decreases in both depression and loneliness. These effects are particularly pronounced for folks who were more depressed when they came into the study."

Hunt suggests that the reason for feeling depressed after spending too much time on social networks boils down to comparison. "When viewing someone else's curated life online, it's easy to see their perfect pictures and think their lives are better than yours." (Hunt, Mental Health Foundation, 2021).

When I hear really smart people, who are studying the topic at length, tell me that the more time someone spends on social media, the more depressed they become, I realize I can fix that, at least for me.

But so many people get caught up in a fear of missing out. The article references the Social Comparison Theory—that we naturally compare our lives to what we see from others. And since most people only want to tell the good and not the bad, and if all you see on social media is good and highly filtered, you begin to think that their life is perfect and yours is not. You believe you are somehow less. That leads to depression which can lead to a very dark and destructive place.

In a 2017 study, Libby Mitchell with the University of Utah asked if the explosion of social media could be the reason for the rise of suicide among young girls to a 40-year high and a 30% rise in suicides among teen boys.

I think that the fact that the question arises, should give us pause. While the research is not conclusive, the timing of the rise with the near domination of social media in the lives of these age groups certainly would suggest a causal link. After all, it is the most likely explanation.

But we can do something about this and reverse this deadly trend. Again, we need to control our inputs and ensure that we are engaging in life-affirming social exchange and not the rest of the junk. Setting a boundary of thirty minutes a day is completely reasonable. I have removed the notifications and moved the Facebook and other social media apps to the back page of my phone. This way I have to work hard to get to it and it becomes less automatic.

After a while, I have stopped thinking about it. Try it. What do you have to lose?

Nothing.

What do you have to gain?

Everything, including your life.

Controlling the Inputs

But what if we flip the script and see the problem of self-esteem, self-worth, and social media differently? What if we can try to work through the problem of the way see and value ourselves? We are smart and by identifying the problem, we know we can overcome it. In working through the challenges of self-esteem and self-worth we can grow stronger and less susceptible to the things that have dragged us down in the past. The key is "because we know we can."

How can we know?

I believe that if we begin with a strong belief in our lives and our value to the world, we can overcome anything. How do we get there? I think we must control the input of messages into our lives and how we view them.

Our lives are shaped by the influences around us; the messages, the examples, the devices we hold in our hands, the books we read or don't read, who we allow into our lives, and so much more.

Many studies provide intriguing results. More than a decade of research on children raised in institutions shows that "neglect is awful for the brain, "said Charles Nelson, professor of pediatrics at Harvard Medical School and Boston Children's. Without someone who is a reliable source of attention, affection, and stimulation, he says, "the wiring of the brain goes awry." The result can be long-term mental and emotional problems. (Nelson, 2014). If we do not have the right kind of care while a child, things can go bad.

Sometimes young people up through adulthood don't fare any better, even if they did have great parents. I believe what we allow into our minds will have either a positive influence or a negative effect on us. So, which one will we select? Which ones will we amplify and which ones will be turned off?

The truth is that everyone has an opinion about us, either directly or indirectly. For instance, when a host or hostess at a restaurant takes you to a table, that person will most likely form an opinion about you based upon your looks, dress, your posture, your facial expression or the tone of your voice, or all of it together.

My question is, does their opinion matter? Should it make us feel better or worse? What if their opinion is colored by their circumstances and a lack of understanding of our circumstances? Can anyone in this place, wherever "this place" may be, have an accurate assessment of you or me? No.

I will say that while the person with the opinion matters, what they think about me is a judgment call on their part and may have little to do with the truth. If they don't know me, it has more to do with their own experiences.

To let that opinion or judgment impact me is to put control of my life and how I feel about myself, into the hands of another who is neither qualified, nor do they have any business there. While we cannot stop their thought process, we can control ours. If we don't, we take ourselves down the path of self-destruction.

But people at a host/hostess stand aren't the only ones with an opinion about us. We should listen to some people in our lives who are significant to us and truly care. When their comments are good, honest, constructive, encouraging, and accurate we should listen. We can improve by being attentive to their wise counsel.

Others who distort, manipulate, and hurt us with their words and actions are not so helpful. Sometimes they communicate in direct conversations, through the spreading of gossip or rumor, social media, or other more subtle but no less real ways.

We need to ask ourselves who we believe. Who do we allow to speak into our lives? Are they qualified? Do they really know us? Why are they sharing, advising, criticizing, or offering to "help?" I say this not to be critical of those who are trying to help but the truth is not all "help" is created equal. Nor is all help, helpful.

So, let's begin with one true statement about our lives today … are you ready?

If I were to speak one true statement about your life today, it would be that **your life matters**.

I do not know your circumstances. I do not know your finances. I do not know your voices, morals, lifestyle, sexual orientation, religion/faith, or anything else about you. And yet, I can say with absolute honesty and great conviction, your life matters.

How can I say that? God made you, on purpose, therefore you matter. I also hope you will take to heart the people mentioned earlier, whose lives prove this truth.

I hope you realize there are things you can do to make it matter even more. But, regardless of what you do from here on out in your life, it matters.

It matters in incalculable ways. It matters to family and friends. It matters to the people you work with. It matters to the charity you give to. It matters to the person you helped the other day, that you didn't know. It matters to the person you encouraged with your words or a helping hand.

But when we allow the negative inputs to crowd out the good, we can become overwhelmed and depressed. When we make choices or allow their opinions to influence how we feel about ourselves, based on that negative input it sets us up for even more pain.

Some advice from the Bob Newhart School of Counseling, "Stop it!" (Just kidding – there is no such thing.)

But we can start today and make different choices. When we feel that something is creating depression or anxiety in our lives, we can actively decide to remove it and move on. I know that this sounds too simplistic, but it is the truth. Just because it is simple, do not discard it—not all things have to be difficult, to be effective.

Let's go to work on ourselves and begin to create a positive self-image.

Dr. Cliff Robertson, Jr.

Chapter 12
Fostering a Positive Self-Image

According to the American Psychiatry Association (APA), "Our self-image is dynamic and changing. Creating and growing a positive self-image is a process that can go on over a lifetime."

What is self-image?

The APA explains that "self-image is the personal view or mental picture, that we have of ourselves. Self-image is an 'internal dictionary' that describes the characteristics of the self, including such things as intelligent, beautiful, ugly, talented, selfish, and kind. These characteristics form our personal paradigm of our assets (strengths) and liabilities (weaknesses) as we see them. It is how you see yourself when you look into the mirror, both the physical mirror and the one in our minds."

How is self-image developed?

"Self-image is a product of learning. Early childhood influences, such as parents and caregivers, have a major influence on our self-image. They are mirrors reflecting an image of ourselves. Our experiences with others such as teachers, friends, and family add to the image in the mirror. Relationships reinforce what we think and feel about ourselves." (APA).

The APA continues, "The image we see in the mirror may be a real or distorted view of who we are. Based on this view, we develop either a positive or a negative self-image. The strengths and weaknesses we have adopted affect how we act today. We continually take in information and evaluate ourselves in several areas, such as physical appearance (How do I look?), performance (How am I doing?), and relationships (How important am I?)."

With a positive self-image, we recognize and own our assets and potentials while being realistic about our liabilities and limitations. With a negative self-image, we focus on our faults and weaknesses, failures and imperfections.

Self-image is important because how we think about ourselves affects how we feel about ourselves and how we interact with others and the world around us. In other words, what are you thinking when you look into the mirror? Are you criticizing and destructive, or are you positive and encouraging?

A positive self-image fostered by the right kind of "self-talk" can make us feel better physically, mentally, emotionally, and spiritually. This can also help our social outlook.

On the other hand, a negative self-image and the negative self-talk that goes with it is just plain destructive in all of these same areas.

How can we create a positive self-image?

Our self-image is not a static thing—once fixed, not always fixed. Our self-image can often swing from good to bad like a metronome.

We must develop a strong and healthy picture of ourselves, thus challenging the distortions in the mirror.

Self-image change occurs over a lifetime. A healthy self-image starts with learning to accept and love ourselves. It also means being accepted and loved by others.

<u>Specific steps to develop a positive self-image</u>

Take a self-image inventory.

Make a list of your positive qualities.

Ask significant others to describe your positive qualities.

Define personal goals and objectives that are reasonable and measurable.

Confront cognitive distortions (aka – Stinking Thinking).

Identify and explore the impact of childhood labels.

Refrain from comparing yourself to others.

Develop your strengths.

Learn to love yourself.

Give yourself positive affirmations and repeat them regularly.

Remember that you are unique.

Remember how far you have come.

YOUR LIFE MATTERS!

<u>What is body image?</u>

Body image is part of self-image. Our body image includes more than what we look like or how others see us. It also refers to how we think, feel, and react to our perception of our physical attributes.

Body image development is affected by cultural images and the influence of family, peers, and others. A positive body image contributes to enhanced psychological adjustment (less depression, positive self-worth, life satisfaction, less interpersonal anxiety, fewer eating disorders). Distortions in our thinking contribute to a negative body image.

How can we enhance our body image?

Body image is not fixed. Our body experiences change as we grow older, and each stage in our life is associated with body image changes. Maintaining a positive body image is a lifelong process.

Changing negative body image means more than changing our bodies. It means changing how we think, feel, and react to our bodies. Learning to have a positive relationship with an imperfect body increases the ability to lose weight. Surgery can be a means for changing how we see ourselves but isn't that still temporary? Extensive outside remodeling also requires extensive inside changes in our body image.

Specific steps to enhance body image:

Explore your personal body image with its strengths and limitations.

Confront thinking distortions related to your body.

Challenge misleading assumptions about body appearance.

Accept and love who you are.

Be comfortable with your body.

Have positive experiences with your body.

Be a friend to your body with positive affirmations.

What are some of the negative things that we say and think about ourselves?

That we are not enough

That we are stupid

That we are poor

That we are ugly/fat

Not enough education

Not enough money

Wrong job/no opportunities to improve – stuck

No one likes me.

I'm a bad person

No one will ever love me

Everyone thinks I'm a loser.

Let's replace those negative thoughts with positive statements.

I am more than enough.

I am beautiful/handsome.

I am improving daily.

I am a good friend.

My weight may not be where I want it, but I am working on it and even if it never changes, I am awesome just the way I am.

Why is it so important to have a Positive Self-Image?

Self-image is a mental picture of the self, the image you make of yourself in your mind, and the ideas you have about your qualities and capacities. Your self-image can come from your experiences, your environment, and even through other people's opinions of you. The collective opinion of yourself is the self-image of your appearance, your position in society, and your worth.

"When a person has a low self-image, then they tend to get shy or even depressed, hiding away from the public. They try to change their appearance by changing everything that they don't like." (Grandself, 2017). Low self-image creates a sense of unworthiness in life and leads to a lack of success and depression.

On the other hand, having a self-image that's too high lends itself to narcissism. Narcissists have so much ego, they believe they are above everyone else.

What is a healthy self-image?

A healthy self-image is balanced. It is based on real-world experience. It does not create a pseudo impression of yourself based on one's fears or others' opinions but a cautiously identified image of the self.

A negative self-image and self-perception are based on a critical judgment of ourselves. This judgment takes the negative side, usually based on a past failure, level of achievement, low-income levels, or a lack of education. It all piles up to portray a negative self-image.

People with a poor self-image will often overcompensate in situations where they fear how society might react to their lowly estate—as they see it. In an effort to hide their flaws from the world, they can become lonely and reclusive.

On the other end of the spectrum, some have an overly inflated, larger-than-life self-perception of themselves. They consider others to be in chaos and destruction when they are the only angels in the world. These are sometimes successful people but have a stingy character that pushes everyone away.

Both ends of the spectrum can be bad.

"Having a balanced self-image is necessary to live a harmonious life." (Grandself, 2017).

A healthy self-image will include

1-Positive outlook on life

Optimism and hope are elements of a proper self-image. A hopeful person has a positive outlook on life, as we discussed in the section on Positive Psychology.

2-Balanced self-image

You are not perfect nor is anyone else. A person with a balanced self-image celebrates success and accepts the loss. They will accept their flaws and see how they can improve them.

3-Healthy self-image does not misunderstand the idea of self-worth but enhances it. Your self-worth is not defined by your success and failures, but by your potential and what you can offer to the world. You have high self-worth because you are a human being and capable of change. Our self-image often affects our sense of self-worth and that is why it is so important that it is

balanced. Many people see their past or even a present failure or mistake as representative of their self-worth as human beings. This can lead to sharp downturns in feelings of self-worth, which can lead to thoughts of suicide. You should not judge your self-worth by what your life looks like today. You are batting 1000% on coming through every difficulty you have faced to date and you will overcome this one too.

Self-image is a creation of our mind. It is our perception of ourselves. Our minds can shape a very different perception of self-image, even if it is far from reality. This can be dangerous.

A case in point involves "a woman who had surgery more than once to remove her long nose. In reality, her nose was so small that the doctor didn't want to do the surgery on her. Even after half of her nose was gone in the first surgery, she wanted to go through the knife for the second time and for the third time." (Grandself, 2017).

Her perceived self-image was not based on reality and she ended up having herself surgically mutilated.

A three-question self-evaluation:

What is my self-image? (Use descriptive language here)

How do I think of myself? (What are your thoughts about you when you are alone?)

How does this self-evaluation make me feel about myself?

List what comes to mind about each question.

As you review your answers, think about these questions.

Do you think you have a healthy self-image? If yes, why?
If no, why?

Write an exhaustive list.

Do you like what you see in the words you have written that describe you? Some of us have a distorted view that is like looking into a cracked mirror. To change the way you view yourself, you must first understand clearly what that view is—what you see in the mirror. I ask again – do you like what you see? If not – which is many of us, then let's see what we can do to change our view of ourselves.

Let's go to work and **create a strong and clear self-image** that reflects your strengths and self-worth without emphasizing the negative. You might have a bad temper or be thirty pounds overweight. Those things can be changed if you are willing to work on them. The only question is your commitment to those changes. With those changes available, you no longer need to create a poor self-image.

Instead, write a statement of your healthy self-image. "I am beautiful. I am currently thirty pounds overweight but that does not define who I am or my self-worth. I will work out three days a week and manage my diet to lose thirty pounds within the next six months. I want to do that because it is negatively affecting my self-image."

Then get busy working on the changes you need to make. Using only your imagination or affirmation will not bring change. If you need education, get it. Go to the gym if your self-image is affected by it. If you are lonely, go make friends by getting involved in organizations that align with who you are and the things that are important to you – like church, non-profits, etc. Work toward your goals as much as you can and you will progress toward your desired outcome.

Remember, your self-image is in your mind. There is not a perfect measure of self-image but having a healthy mind and healthy thoughts will include having a balanced self-image.

Why are these questions important?

These questions are important because they tell us who we think we are. Until we deal with negative thoughts, it will be impossible to think any differently. Cognitive distortions can settle in our minds. Those distortions replay over and over with what the media is saying, what our past is saying, what we think others are saying and what our thoughts about ourselves tell us.

We must learn a new way of processing those cognitive distortions and systematically destroying them. The narrative we create in our head, or that our parents/peers/media create for us, can destroy us. At the very least, those negative thoughts hold us back from experiencing a life that is beyond comparison to anything we can imagine.

~

Your life matters.

What happens when we get this wrong?

I have become a student of life and for life. Every day I listen to something to help me grow as a person, a husband, a father, and as a professional. I haven't always done this but I'm sure glad I started. I believe that this is what started me down this path to write this book and produce a podcast soon.

So far, I have shared a lot of stories. Many were positive, but not all. Sometimes life just doesn't go the way we want it to. What are we to do then?

I want to share the story of a titan of industry. At one point he was listed among the richest men in the world. An innovator, strategist, and investor, his companies created life-saving drugs. He created new and improved medicines for the future.

This man was worth billions until the economy took a nosedive in 2008. This worldwide financial crisis crippled banks and stock markets around the globe. He was no longer the wealthiest man in Germany, which had been a huge source of pride for this Corporate Giant.

He applied for loans for his company. Because of the challenging times, they warned him the loans may not get approved. He tried a risky investment that he was sure would pay off, but it was a great failure. He went from a net worth of over twelve billion to nine billion.

Distraught over the financial situation and the investment loss, on January 5, 2009, he took his life. The day after his death, the company was informed that the loans had been approved. His name? Adolph Merkle of Merkle Pharmaceutical.

He thought that his life no longer mattered. He believed he was worthless to humanity and had failed beyond words. The humiliation was more than he could take.

He failed to recognize his company was saving lives, helping people live longer. He lost sight of the fact that he was not in financial ruin but could have self-funded the loans to his company if he had to, and recouped them later. He had enough to live on for a hundred lifetimes. Mr. Merkle had created a distorted view of reality for himself, and the depression death spiral that followed was beyond his capacity to pull out of.

While most of us cannot fathom being a billionaire, losing billions, or even creating a company that saves lives, we have all taken a hit to our ego. Negative turns in the economy have impacted us all. There have been times when we have been genuinely worried about the future – our financial future and our lives. This worry can lead to anxiety. This anxiety, untended to, can lead to despair and depression. Sometimes this depression can be so overwhelming, that we think that the only answer is to end our lives. We believe—in error— the world would be better off without us.

Nothing could be further from the truth.

When you are going through tough times, I challenge you to find a friend to talk with who will encourage you. Sometimes we simply don't have an accurate picture of the world around us and we need a different perspective. I have been worried about this or that at times and my wife would challenge my thinking, setting me back on the right path. Or I could call a friend, and he would have a positive word of encouragement that lifted the weight of worry from my shoulders. We need those true voices to speak into our lives. I believe that if Adolph Merkle had done that, he would still be with us today. I believe that many others would be as well.

Maybe your rough time is so hard you need professional help. Seek it out.

They are available and ready to help.

Suicide is a permanent solution to a temporary problem. Mr. Merkle's problems were over the very next day.

Once you have found someone to talk with, I further challenge you to get out of your house and do something for someone else. Remember earlier in the book when I gave flowers to strangers at Wal-Mart? It changed my whole outlook at the time.

Go ahead and plan to do something for someone else at least twice a week.

Then I want you to begin to journal. It doesn't matter if you use a notepad, your phone, or a fancy journal book. Write about your day, beginning with the five things that you are grateful for that day. After that, write whatever is on your mind and heart. Looking for the good, and imagine the hope in a better day. The Bible tells us that hope comes in the morning.

I would also like to invite you to schedule time for exercise three or four times a week. Walking is a good choice, but you might choose another option. Whatever physical exercise you choose will release chemicals in your brain and body that will significantly elevate your sense of well-being.

Finally, I want you to <u>read or meditate on something sacred—like Scripture, daily</u>. I am not trying to make you a "Holy Roller," nor am I trying to convert you to something that you do not believe in. That is way beyond my capacity and paygrade.

I do, however, know from research that this practice, along with the other things I have listed here, will have a profound impact on your sense of well-being, and happiness. I use *Our Daily Bread* and *The Word for You Today*. The first one is free and the other is paid. There are many other options out there, find one that's right for you.

To be honest, these are things we need to be doing in both good times and bad. I believe that it creates an almost bullet-proof sense of self. In my experience, when tough times come, this personal system of self-care becomes a lifeline that restores me to positive mental health. Research has proven that it does.

In addition, I want you to find two or three people you can talk to and encourage, who are encouraging to you as well. If you are married, then one of them needs to be your spouse. I realize that all relationships are different, so ultimately this is your decision. The two or three people need to be positive and honest with you, just as you are with them. These are people that will be there for you in the best of times or the worst of times, and you will be there for them as well. These people can be your lifeline when you feel all hope is lost.

One of the worst things in this life is to feel like we are all alone and that no one cares about us. When we isolate ourselves from others, it is like we are digging a pit for ourselves to dwell in. At first, we're comfortable there because there is no one to criticize or look down on us. But it's not long before those walls begin to close in. The loneliness—often followed by hopelessness and despair—can become overwhelming.

If you do not have these people in your life, you can fix that. Get involved with a volunteer group helping the homeless, a pregnancy help center, or Habitat for Humanity building a home for someone. You can also get involved in a church small group. Try one. If the first one doesn't feel right, try the next one and the next one until you find one that works for you. This is important.

One last thought. Your life matters, whether you believe that it does or not. The impact your life makes on this world can't be calculated in dollars and cents but in lives that have been touched. Create this routine for yourself and I believe that regardless of what happens, you will find your way back to wellness.

Dr. Cliff Robertson, Jr.

Chapter 13

Your Life has a Purpose. Discover it Now.

You were created for a purpose that only you can fulfill. The true purpose of your life boils down to one question. What is the reason you get up in the morning?

Your purpose, which could also be referred to as a calling, can guide your life choices, direct your behavior, assist in the creation of goals, lead you in the direction of your dreams, and help give your life true meaning. For many of us, our purpose is tied to our work. For others, their purpose is discovered in family or friends, through acts of service or caring.

Each person's purpose will be unique to them and them alone. Most often, we find that over the years of our lives, our purpose may evolve into something completely different than it is today—and that is to be expected.

(The following scenarios were borrowed from an article produced by the University of Minnesota, Center for Spirituality and Healing, Dr. Barb Leonard, 2016.) Questions that may come up when you reflect upon your life's purpose might include:

Who am I?

Where do I belong?

When do I feel fulfilled?

163

What makes me happy?

Consider Mary. "I have a job as a legal aide, which is pretty interesting and pays fairly well. But my real love is music. I love to play my cello, and I practice a few hours a day. I especially love to perform for others and bring beauty to a special occasion, like a wedding."

So, who is Mary? Is she a legal aid or cellist?

Sometimes in life, we play multiple roles. But to define ourselves by the roles we play, whether it is a work role, family role, or even a role as a volunteer, I think falls short of who we are.

The truth is, Mary is a beautiful woman who has a passion for the beauty of music and loves to help others. Now, I have no idea what Mary looks like in person, but she is beautiful because she is God's creation. That is the core of who she is—a beautiful creation of God.

Her roles may define how she expresses herself—like a legal aide, a person who helps others with legal issues. She may need to do that for her income, or until her passion as a cellist can grow to a point where it pays for her livelihood.

Your job may not necessarily be fulfilling your heart. I am not sure it is always meant to. I think we fulfill who we are by the way we express our love. For Mary, that involves music. It may never earn her enough to quit her day job, but that's fine. Everyone's path is different and that was hers.

But what if you know you are called to something, like becoming a full-time musician? What are you supposed to do with that?

If this is your driving passion, find someone else who has done what you are wanting to do. See how they accomplished that life mission. Then map out what you have to do to make that happen.

It is going to require sacrifice and work that is probably harder than you ever imagined you are capable of. Even then, it may not happen. But then again, it certainly can. At least by doing it this way, you give yourself the best chance to make your dreams come true.

Rick is another case study. "A few years ago, my father was very sick in the hospital. I was so impressed by the nurses there and how they made such a difference to my father and our family that I decided that I wanted to have a job like that. So, I went to nursing school, and now I work as an RN in a local clinic."

Sometimes, like Rick, we discover our life mission in places that we never even considered before. I believe that this comes from an open heart that is seeking, even when it doesn't know what it is looking for.

Over my life, I have had several different jobs. Some were out of necessity, while others were out of passion. Other jobs came to be because God opened a door that I didn't know existed. What doors appear to be opening for you?

Your life purpose is ...

Most people are reluctant to pursue their life purpose because they worry that it sounds self-serving or might be a selfish quest. However, your true purpose is about recognizing who you are, along with your unique gifts, and putting them to work to make the world a better place. It could be playing beautiful music for others to enjoy, helping friends solve problems, giving to a cause that sparks a passion inside you, or simply bringing more joy into the lives of those around you through encouraging words and thoughtful acts of grace.

Something you need to know about YOU

There is no one else on the planet like you. You are one of a kind and we are blessed and honored to know and love you.

Some people ask, what does how your body design say about you and your value?

Some are born with diseases that adversely impact their capacity to do certain things. Does this diminish their value?

No.

God tells us that we all have a purpose and that purpose is seen in His strength at work through us, not our strength alone. I believe this means that we need to look beyond our greatest challenges and see the gifts.

I shared some stories earlier about how some people not only overcame their disabilities but ended up doing more in their lives than people who are not disabled.

What are the things that you do that make you happy?

I asked myself this question the other day and I had to think about it for a minute. I mean, I am generally a happy person but what is it I do that makes me happy?

As I began to explore this idea, I found that simple things make me happy—snuggling with my wife, traveling and seeing new things, playing golf, working out, writing, speaking, and helping others.

But then I had to ask myself why am I not doing more of these things that make me happy? The only things on this list that I do regularly are snuggle with my wife and work out. I need and want to write more, speak more, travel more, etc. I guess it's time to make some changes in my own life.

What about you? Make a list of four to five things that make you happy.

_____

_____

_____

_____

_____

These things matter in this world because you matter. The happier you are, the more it positively impacts others.

I experience joy in the things I do.

I challenge you to seek joy in all you do. If you can't find the joy in it, maybe it isn't something you need to be doing, at least not long-term.

I watched a video the other day by Robin Sharma about a bathroom attendant at the Johannesburg International Airport, in South Africa. This man had the perfect attitude about his job. His bathroom was his office and he was an ambassador to everyone who came in, welcoming them to his beautiful country. He had found joy in all that he was doing—including cleaning up a bathroom where hundreds of people visited every day. If he found joy in his work, can't we find joy in ours?

What many will miss is that this man is changing the world around him daily for the good. You can do the same thing, regardless of where you are.

I provide for my family by working and seeking to make my home a safe, secure place. Doing those two simple things creates a better world for my family/friends. This includes safety and security - physically, financially, emotionally, and spiritually.

It doesn't matter whether you are the lowest person on the company org – chart or the CEO, you are important. Just by doing the things that you do daily, often without even thinking about it, you make a difference in this world. This world is a better place because of you.

Here is something I want you to do.

I want you to say the following positive affirmation statements every day.

Then I want you to do them—take the action in the statement.

Positive Affirmation - *I grow intellectually, emotionally, physically, and spiritually daily.*

To grow intellectually, we must read or listen to books or educational podcasts.

To grow emotionally, we must connect to our hearts and express those emotions in healthy ways to those we love. We can also grow this area of our life through journaling about what is going on in our lives and making a daily gratitude top five list.

To grow in physical strength, we need to be committed to our health, including a positive diet and exercise routine, as we are able.

To grow spiritually, we need to be connecting to God, through His word and prayer daily. If you don't know where to start, I suggest one devotional that I follow. Download the *Our Daily Bread* app. It's free. It provides a daily thought, Scripture, and prayer. It's a simple and effective way to start your spiritual growth.

Positive Affirmation - *I create a career path that I excel in – and this makes me feel good about myself.*

There are so many times that we are doing a job that we do not enjoy but we do it to pay the bills. You may feel like you don't have any other options, but that isn't true

First - Find the joy in where you are.

Second - Define what you want your career to look like and utilize your current job as a launching pad for that future. Explore school options. A lot of financial aid options are out there. Explore online classes that give you the flexibility to do classes on your schedule. No one has ever said, "I wish I didn't have so much education."

Third – Invest in yourself. The bottom line is to stick to your dream and the plan. It will require work and lots of discipline, but every step will matter and help you to get to where you want to go. Warren Buffet once said, "The best investment you can make, is an investment in yourself … The more you learn, the more you earn."

More things to remember…

You matter in your home.

One of the things that I have discovered in this journey, is that it is not so much how much you have to say, but how well you listen to those whom you love. The better I become at listening, the better life becomes for all around me. When I recognize the words of those whom I love by reflecting them back to them, the more they open up and want to share. The love that this creates, is beyond understanding.

When we listen to understand, instead of preparing our response, we listen and connect to the ones who love us on a whole different level.

In this way, we matter. Our presence is significant to our loved ones. They long to have someone they can be their authentic self with and unload the pain of the day, week, month, year, or more.

They also want someone to hear them and know them on a deeper level.

By listening to them, their sense of personal significance grows. They realize they matter. With that, their appreciation of you grows. It will be visible as they express how much you matter to them.

The bottom line is that the more we let people know
that they matter to us,
that they are significant,
and that we care,
the more we matter to them.
It has a multiplying effect on our world.

Strive to make a difference by being a good listener.

Your intelligence and wisdom matter.

As we already noted, when we care for others, they want to know us and hear what we have to say. There is a saying, "no cares what you know until they know how much you care."

But when people know you care, because you have become an intentional listener, they will want to hear from you. Everything on your mind matters to them. Your wisdom becomes like a well-spring of life to them. Your intellect becomes a light into their future, revealing possibilities for them they never knew existed.

171

Who knows? You might have gone through or are currently going through something that's exactly what they need to hear. It could give them hope to get through their situation. You might have learned something that they need to know. It could be something you read, or heard in a classroom, at work, or just in the process of living life.

I don't know how many times someone has told me, "I have never heard that before ... how did you learn that?"

Then I share where it came from and often in that conversation there is more to learn and share. This is another reason we must be lifelong learners. As we grow, we can help those around us grow. When we do, we are making the world a better place. That's a life that matters.

Your acts of caring matter.

When the Boy Scout helps the elderly lady across the street it matters. When someone holds a door open for others, it matters. Even when no one notices, it matters.

How do you treat someone in a drive-through? Recently, I became distracted and almost completely ignored the person serving. When my wife called me out on it, I felt horrible. Since then, I've been going out of my way to thank the person who has a thankless job.

A young lady working at the local Sonic drive-thru window was new to the job and nervous, but she was trying so hard. She was smiling behind her mask, but her eyes told me she was struggling.

So, I told her that she was doing a great job. Her voice changed, and I could hear the smile I couldn't see. She lowered her mask and gave me the biggest smile she could.

You would have thought I'd just given her a million dollars. All I did was to care, intentionally, about someone. It took only a few seconds and a few words. I wonder how those words impacted her and everyone else she encountered for the rest of the day. Maybe a hundred people came to her window later that day and received a smile with their order. Caring enough to be nice to someone serving you can make a huge impact, not just on your service but on the service of everyone else.

How many times do you care like this in small ways? I once heard Robin Sharma tell about something he does when he goes out to eat. He buys a bottle of wine and gets one glass full. Then he has the waiter or waitress take the bottle back to the kitchen for the kitchen staff to share. It's his way of saying thanks for the amazing work they do. I imagine the kitchen staff never forgets it.

Maybe that is beyond your financial ability. That's okay. But what about a simple thank you, smile, or acknowledgment? Just knowing that someone noticed and appreciated your efforts can make a huge difference in their world. You might check on someone who is feeling under the weather or just seems down. There are a hundred ways that you can, and probably do, care for others daily. Many may have become so automatic for you that you don't notice anymore, but each one of them matters.

You matter in school/work/and more.

Your interaction in class and with others, your insights or questions all matter. At work, someone else might not be able to do their job until you do yours. The product you deliver might make someone else's life easier, healthier, or safer.

The income you create impacts others and yourself by providing money for infrastructure or jobs in the service or retail sector. The livelihood in your part of the world is enhanced because of you.

When you think, "I am depressed and no one cares, because I do not matter," you are wrong.

Often, people will suffer from depression in silence. The lie we tell ourselves is that no one cares and that the world would be a better place without us. This spirals us even further down an ever-darkening hole where we feel there is no way out.

But if we reach out and talk with someone about it, we find that there are people who care. Some people have experienced exactly what we are going through and may be able to help us through it.

We will likely find others who are going through a similar struggle at the same time. The fact that you and they are not alone in this challenge may be lifesaving for each of you.

If you feel it is so bad or hopeless that you can't talk with anyone, don't believe that lie. Reach out to a counselor or a pastor you trust. Talk with them, and I believe it will help. Do not suffer in silence. Get the help you need and deserve. Yes, I said "deserve" because you are valuable. You deserve help. Your life matters.

Fear can derail your purpose.

I love the passage in the Bible that says you were not given the spirit of fear but of power, of love, and a sound mind. 2 Timothy 1:7 This means that you are a warrior, to fight the good fight for the best life. You were not given the spirit of fear but of power. But still, fear slips in.

I hear you. I battle with it too.

So many times, we're afraid of what others think. We're afraid to try something because we might fail. We're afraid to finish something because we fear being judged for it. We fear loss or losing control. We can experience fear over almost everything.

What's interesting is that most of what we're afraid of never happens. Ever. When we live in fear, we develop a deer-in-the-headlights mentality and become frozen, afraid to move. However, action is the thing that can alleviate our fear.

So why do we let fear rule, wreck and ruin our lives?

We've all been afraid.

Fear makes us feel different, alone, embarrassed, or ashamed. Some may become angry, defensive, or hostile. Throughout human history, fear has driven our actions and our unwanted emotions.

Fear fuels our behavior, such as anxiety, PTSD, and aggression. (ADAA, 2017).

As a society, fear-based movements have been unethical, inhumane, and destructive. Ironically, fear, which exists for our survival, might be the strongest emotional driver of risk for our self-destruction as a species.

Why is the emotion of fear so strong? All mammals share a similar neural circuitry for processing threats. The fear reflex is arguably the strongest of primitive survival instincts. But, can our fears be controlled?

"In recent years, neuroscientists have made amazing advancements in our understanding of the role of the amygdala, the best-known brain area underlying the fear response, and its interactions with other regulatory brain components. Specific individual cell populations that are intermingled within the amygdala appear to relay fear-on vs. fear-off behavioral pathways." (ADAA, 2017).

The science is interesting. They continue to gather scientific information. Meanwhile, there are ways to overcome our fears. There are small steps we can take every day.

Looking back at the 2 Timothy verse, remember the three things God has already given us; power, love, and a sound mind.

Power, I believe, is the gift God gives us to step into the fear we feel and overcome it.

Louis E. Boone said, "You gain strength, courage, and confidence by every experience in which you stop to look fear in the face." Each time you step into your fear, you grow. It is said that sailors never learn their trade-in calm seas. They have to be tested in rough seas and it can be fearful.

If they allowed fear to freeze them in their tracks, it could lead to a deadly outcome. When they step into their fear and face the storm, the ship—which is built for the storm, as are you—will thrive. You will too.

Love. Sometimes we are afraid of being hurt, so we withhold our love. We think we are protecting ourselves when we do this but the truth is that we are now hurting two people.

Sometimes we withhold love, in a service capacity because we feel that it will put us in a compromising and dangerous situation. We do need to be wise, but in doing so we can accurately weigh the best options and take our fear out of the equation.

If it is truly a dangerous setting, it might be possible to devise a work-around where you can still show love to the people in need without exposing yourself to the danger. Ultimately, love always wins, when we do not let fear rule our hearts and minds.

Sound Mind. James F. Byrnes said, "Of all the liars in the world, sometimes the worst are our own fears."

John C. Maxwell said, "Nothing in life is to be feared, it is only to be understood. Now is the time to understand more, so that we may fear less."

The idea of a sound mind is pretty simple. Apply the intelligence we are given to navigate the situation—whatever it may be. We may not know exactly what to do, but if we will take a moment and process it, we will discover that the answer is there.

"Woman, thou art loosed," is the phrase Jesus used in the biblical story of a woman who struggled for 18 years with a crippling disability. The Bible identifies the source of the crippling disability as an evil spirit. She couldn't even stand up straight.

I've wondered if the disability that had her bent over was a physical or emotional one. I believe it was an emotional disability that led to a physical expression of being bent over.

How many times do we have something going on in our lives from an emotional place? Depression, anxiety, grief, destructive and toxic relationships all may begin to express themselves in our physical health. According to medical experts, the effects of depression alone can wreak havoc on the body leading to insomnia, migraines, and fatigue. In addition, it can lead to chronic pain and increased risk of heart disease, among other things.

Anxiety carries a whole array of physical impacts as well. I have heard stories of anxiety attacks that feel like and have all the symptoms of a heart attack. Anxiety can become debilitating and so chronic that it makes us unable to function in social settings, do our jobs, and lose any hint of happiness.

Emotional struggles can lead to a diminished quality of life.

So, what do you do about it? Well, one of Jesus' names was Wonderful Counselor. Find someone you can talk to that is trained to help with the issues that you are facing. If paying for a professional counselor is beyond your capacity, there are non-profit counseling services available, along with churches.

Find someone you trust to help you walk out of this challenging time. It is not a sign of weakness to need help. It means you are human. All of us need help from time to time.

Some of the greatest people the world has ever known had emotional and mental health struggles. They sought help and it made all the difference.

Let's deal with the past now by talking about it. Once we work through that, let's celebrate the hero that you are. I want you to get out of the house and engage in activities that matter; volunteer organizations, veteran's organizations, church groups, other civic service organizations, and continue to make a difference.

If this isn't something you can do, I want you to get outside in nature and the sunshine, surrounding yourself with the beautiful things that God has created. Learn something new by visiting a nursery. Pick out some new plants to bring home and get your hands in the dirt. Then reach out to a loved one over the phone or through a handwritten note, letting them know how much they are appreciated and loved.

Let's change your narrative into one that sounds like, "I am important. I have value. I have more to offer to the fabric of life that I can ever fully realize but want to enjoy the process of discovery."

If you don't believe it yourself, let's get a second, third or fourth opinion. There are options. You have so much life to live and give.

I want you to begin by writing your story down on paper. This might be just for you because you don't know anyone who will read it. But one of your children, grandchildren, or someone else down the road would like to know more about what your life was like.

Spend time with your kids, grandkids, and relatives. Give them more of you. They will be richer for the experience, and you will feel connected to them in a way that will add to your life. Your life will overflow with richness and you will come to understand that your life matters.

For those that have no living family, spending time with others that share your interests, hobbies, or passions can create that same richness. I know that many people enjoy participating in reading programs at elementary schools. The bottom line is that we are richer as we seek to enrich the lives of others.

Honestly, what matters here is not how we do it, but that we find ways to do the best we can to serve others. In doing this, we change the world around us. Do not limit yourself to just my suggestions – I often struggle here too.

Even today, I struggled with "is this message, this book, enough? Am I missing something that is even more important?"

So, I brainstormed about other paths and messages, and it seemed to only regurgitate someone else's words. That wasn't for me and I couldn't get excited about that at all.

I asked myself, "what am I passionate about? What moves me? What do people need to hear that is going to make a difference for them?"

But I had to stop and take a counseling call. As I was talking with this young man, he shared his battle with depression. He couldn't see any purpose in his life.

While he unloaded his emotional pain of depression and hopelessness, I empathized with him, because I too have battled with depression.

I asked him, "What do you do to help others?"

He said, "Well, I set up chairs at the church I go to every Sunday. A little over a hundred and fifty of them."

I replied, "So you touch, through service about three hundred people a month?"

He agreed.

Then I asked him about his job. "How many people do you work with as an insurance adjuster each month, on average?"

He told me, "Between sixty to a hundred and twenty."

"So all in all, you impact between three hundred-sixty to four hundred-twenty people each month in a positive way?"

He said, "I guess so."

Then I said, "Okay. Let's do something here. In church, those numbers are pretty static. You are also encountering another

181

twenty or more people a day like store clerks, other employees, and friends and family. So if we did the math on sixty people through work that's seven hundred twenty each year. If we use two months of the church numbers, that's six hundred people. Then we add the twenty per day for five days a week for fifty-two weeks. That's five thousand, two hundred people."

"So, between the three numbers, you have a positive impact on sixty-four hundred people or more per year. That's a life that matters. But let's put this into another perspective. In four years, that would equal over twenty-four thousand people, enough to fill the Staples Center in Los Angeles to overflowing or Madison Square Gardens. If we look at it over eleven years, you could fill almost every major football stadium in the United States."

"Imagine for a moment an arena like the Staples Center or a stadium the size of Soldier Field, Arrowhead, or NRG, filled to capacity with people who were cheering for you because of the positive impact that you had on them? Close your eyes and think about that for just a moment. It is overwhelming."

When I shared this with my client, he was brought to tears. I told him to put it in the context of the movie, *It's a Wonderful Life* and to consider himself as the George Bailey character.

He told me that this was the best he had felt in years. He began to dream again and see beyond his current circumstances, and it changed his life.

It can do the same for you.

When I was a young man and attending a church youth group, we looked at what others were doing to see how we might be motivated to do something ourselves.

I was intrigued by a story of a young preacher from Pennsylvania. He served God in his calling and then one day he picked up a *Life* magazine and read about a gang of young men, teenagers, who were on trial for murder. Growing up in rural America, it was hard for him to believe something like that was happening, yet it was in living color on the pages before him. Something about it stirred his soul.

When he prayed, he heard God speak to him clearly saying, "Go to those boys!"

He wasn't sure what to do with this revelation or where to go but he was certain God had just told him to go.

So, he found out the location of the trial and drove to New York. He found the courthouse and went in for the proceedings, with the feeling he needed to reach out to them, somehow. When the courtroom was emptying for the day, he tried to go forward and talk with the boys to tell them he loved them, God loved them, and that Jesus died for them.

The boys were shocked. Some scoffed. The police escorted this young preacher from the courtroom roughly and told him to keep his distance from the "dangerous hoodlums."

The press caught wind of it and approached to take pictures and ask questions. The police stepped back, and the preacher just raised his Bible a bit. The picture made the headlines in the New

York newspapers the next day, with the story of a young preacher who had come, at God's calling, to help the gangs of New York.

While some laughed at the audacity of it all, some saw it as an answer to prayer. A few of the gang members had been watching from the gallery. One of them realized the preacher was different. In the past, most people had ridiculed them and told them how bad they were and needed to be punished, usually emphasizing that they were all going to hell. No one ever seemed to care about them, except this guy. They wondered who he was and why he cared so much.

They didn't have to wait long for their answer. That night he searched for them. He found out where they hung out and walked down there, to find them.

He approached a young man who he thought might be one of the gang members. The "young man" turned out to be just a boy, no more than ten or twelve. He had a look of fear in his eyes, but it quickly turned to a defiant glare.

Thinking the preacher was a policeman coming to give his friends a hard time, he yelled at him. One of the older boys who saw him in the courtroom that day recognized the preacher and told the younger boy to back down, this was not a cop.

The preacher introduced himself as David and the boys brought him to their 'gang house.' David asked about each of them. Their stories of trouble and tragedy broke his heart.

One of them asked, "Hey Preach, you told our boys today in court that God loved them. Is that true? Cuz you see, everyone else tells us that God is going to get us."

This opened the door for David to share about Jesus with them. Some seemed eager to hear more, while others smirked and laughed.

The preacher was not deterred. He went back to the trial the next day and then to the gang house afterward. He didn't preach to them. He cared about them. Slowly, even the doubters in the gang began to soften.

One of the gang members had a girlfriend with a serious heroin addiction. She asked him for money to buy some "junk"—slang for the drug.

He told her that if she will "get rid of the preacher," he would buy her all the drugs she could use.

The preacher's wife had joined him in New York a couple of weeks after he first came. The girl found the two of them walking on the street and approached them, but she couldn't go through with it. She broke down and sobbed in front of them. The pastor's wife embraced her and they took the broken girl back to the chapel house where they stayed.

Severe heroin withdrawal symptoms came on the girl, but the pastor and his wife stayed with her and nursed her back to health. After she sobered, Rosa became their ally.

Meanwhile, in "GangLand" the Mau Maus and the rival gang, the Bishops, were about to battle for turf, respect, and the revival meeting that David had going.

Something happened that Nicki, the Mau Maus leader didn't expect. When he heard David's message, God touched his heart. He called off the fight and gave his heart to Christ.

Many others gave their hearts to Christ not only that night but in the coming days. A "great exchange" took place where the gang members traded their weapons, mostly bats and switchblades, for Bibles.

If the story ended there, it would be miraculous enough, but it didn't. David and Nicki, who became an ordained minister, started a place for young boys to escape gang life and drugs, Teen Challenge, in New York. This took place in the late fifties and early sixties. Now it's an international ministry that serves men and women, teens and adults. It has been life-changing. World-changing.

And to think it all started because one young man from a rural part of the country was moved to take action. There's no telling how many people have been touched by the ministry of David Wilkerson. You might have heard of the book and movie about it, *The Cross and the Switchblade.*

The ministry is still changing lives today. Ten years after the founders passing, it's now called, Adult-Teen Challenge. I've had the opportunity to work with them on several occasions and they are the real deal.

Maybe there is something or someone you feel called to help. Do it. It could change the world.

Joyce Meyers

What would you think if I told you about someone who grew up in an abusive home where she was sexually molested from the age of five until she left her house upon graduation from high school? How do you think her story turned out?

What if I were to tell you that this young lady, to escape the sexual abuse, moved out and married the first guy who showed any interest in her? This part-time used car salesman convinced his new bride to steal from the company she worked from so that they could go on vacations to California.

Sounds like a woman on a fast track to prison, right? Add to that, they frequented bars and drank heavily. The husband, during all of his free time, cheated on his wife.

After five years of this, she had caught him one too many times. She walked out and they divorced.

She knew she needed a different life and went to church. As she became involved, she ended up teaching a women's Bible study. She met a man at church, and they dated for a year or so before they married.

Her life headed in a new direction. Her Bible study grew popular, and after a few years, she became the associate pastor of the growing church. She was asked to do a daily fifteen-minute inspirational radio spot.

Letters and notes came from people who commented on how her message and teaching was exactly what they had needed to hear at that moment. Some wrote from broken homes and broken marriages. Others were writing from the brink of suicide and sharing that her messages had saved their lives.

She eventually started an independent ministry with the radio program and it went to radio stations all over that part of the country. When that happened, she stepped down from the church to focus on this full-time ministry. She sold tapes of her messages at different churches where she spoke and wrote a book that became popular.

One day her husband commented, "You should start a TV program. I bet that would help a lot of people."

WGN in Chicago picked up her show, *Enjoying Everyday Living*, with Joyce Meyers.

She went from someone who suffered abuse as a child for a very long time, to someone traveling and ministering around the globe. Her books have sold millions of copies. Her fans will tell you that her message is relatable and personal. Some mention that her stories of abuse, ugly marriage, and then total transformation by Christ, have helped them through some of the toughest times in their lives, in some cases, literally saving their lives.

This is more than a rags to riches story. Her story is to inspire those who are going through really tough times right now. You may be thinking that there is no hope. You may believe that the things you have done, are beyond redemption.

You would be wrong.

You may be thinking you don't know where to begin. Well, here are some ideas.

Remember my story about going to Wal-Mart and buying a plant or flowers for someone, anyone? What did Joyce do that turned her life around?

She got involved with something that lifted her and inspired her to give to others. She didn't know she was going to end up where she is today, but knowing she needed something different, she took that step of faith to a new place—a positive step that changed everything about her life.

It could have the same result for you. Get involved with a cause, maybe several. Go back to school. Find a church. Do something positive and affirming and see where it leads you. Make sure you are giving to those around you as you go, When you do that, you're planting seeds for your future.

You do not know when or where the harvest will come, but rest assured it will come and it will be life-changing for you and all who know you, not to mention all of those that you gave to along the way.

Now don't get me wrong. You don't have to give money. Joyce began by giving of her time as a volunteer Bible study teacher. She learned the lesson and taught it. She didn't have a formal education, so don't let that be something that holds you back, either.

Erin and Ben Napier

Many have heard of Erin and Ben Napier from the hit HGTV show, *Hometown*. Erin posted on Instagram while they were in the process of renovating their 1925 Craftsman cottage dream home on a budget.

But this isn't about stardom and how you get there. It's about how we matter. What they did in their hometown of Laurel, Mississippi, changed the world for many people in that town. Laurel, not that many years ago was pretty rundown, like many small towns in America today. Locals had moved out, industries relocated, and the town was withering on the vine.

Ben and Erin, along with several friends and relatives decided they were going to do something about it and they did. Taking on one house or building at a time, they transformed much of their town into something pretty special. What's even more extraordinary is how the changes they started have cascaded into an economic boom for the whole town.

My wife and I traveled there recently, and we were blown away to see it all. We were there in the middle of the week and all of the restaurants were busy, some with waiting lines outside. The shops were busy. The main street was shining like a new dime. A lot of work was still in progress, but you could see that tremendous change had taken place and it was only growing. It was inspiring, to say the least.

A couple of things to note here, as the Ben & Erin company name grew, they kept as much of their product and order fulfillment local as possible. They employ over fifty locals, not including film and production crews from HGTV. They've created good jobs for people, providing a boost to the local economy and the economic base of the area.

If they had farmed it out overseas, it would have helped their pocketbooks but not helped the community. This people over profit mentality tells me that these people are special. They would rather make less and impact more.

This also tells me they value people. You and me. I also see it in the homes they choose to renovate and show on TV. It's most often the affordable home that they are working on and not the super expensive. Now don't get me wrong, once or twice a season, you will see a higher-end home thrown in there but even then, it is still not extravagant.

I am not here to make Ben and Erin heroes. I'm saying the lives of the people in Laurel and the surrounding areas matter to them. They do a lot for the people of this area. They give. This is a testament to me of what one couple can do if they care for others in a real, tangible way.

I recently read an article about one of the houses that they renovated on their show. The couple who lived there are moving away as part of a work advancement and the house is for sale. The realtor who has the home listed told the reporter that he gets calls nearly every day from people looking to move there from all over the country because they want to be a part of what is going on in Laurel, MS.

I wonder how you and I might do this where we are today? I wonder if we helped a neighbor or got involved in our local town revitalization efforts what difference could it make. How many people it could lift? We would tell them "Your Life Matters" without ever saying the words, just showing them by our actions. I think this might just change the world.

Tony Robbins

His life started in a pretty tough environment with an abusive, even violent home life. When his mom left her husband, Tony's life got better.

She remarried and the new husband adopted Tony as his son. They didn't make a lot of money. Tony worked as a night janitor while he was in school so that they could pay for food and electricity. When he turned eighteen, he left home but stayed at the same job. His work skills didn't allow for much else.

Then he met someone who recommended this self-improvement workshop by a guy named Jim Rhone. It cost around $50.00 to attend. Tony managed to scrape up the money and went.

It changed his life.

He went on to promote Jim Rhone conferences and Jim took Tony under his wing, mentoring him. The rest, as they say, is history.

Tony Robbins became wildly successful, but I don't want to focus on that. I want to look at someone who started with nothing, became something, and now spends most of his time working to help others. Too many times, we only focus on the "overnight success" part of the story. A person got a break that we didn't get.

When the truth is, Tony cleaned toilets for a living to eat until his breakthrough came. He worked hard and did the thankless work that many in America do as well. He did not allow his circumstances to dictate who he was or what his potential could be. He didn't allow his socio-economic status to determine his value or his future.

Now fast forward forty years, Tony is very successful. Yet, to me, what makes him worth writing about, is not the money he has made or the businesses he has built, but how much he has given to help those in most dire need.

As his career took off, he began The Tony Robbins Foundation to help youth in crisis, the homeless, the hungry, the elderly, and those in prison. In 2014 he donated the proceeds of his books, *Money, Master the Game,* and *Unshakable*, to Feeding America.

Above and beyond the book royalties, he donated more money to the charity out of his pocket. In addition, Tony works with an organization called Spring Health to provide much-needed clean drinking water to rural parts of India. He is also involved with a non-profit called, Operation Underground Railroad, which is focused on ending human trafficking. His work is not just changing lives but saving lives.

I find these missions incredible. But in all of this, what you don't see is that behind the scenes, even from his earliest days,

Tony focused on helping those that couldn't help themselves. When someone was in need, and he could help, he helped. His life mattered to many, even before he had what the world would call "wealth." After he obtained wealth, he continued his mission of helping those who were in dire need.

While that is remarkable, I also see that he often gave when he was at his lowest, either financially or emotionally. Like most people, he battled with depression at times. He discovered that by helping others, his mental health improved.

Isn't it funny that our greatest challenges can lead us to a place of healing, as we turn to help others? This just seems to round out the message that our lives—wherever we are—matter.

We don't have to be a Tony Robbins to change the world. We can do it from wherever we are, one person at a time. In fact, we are probably already doing it and don't even realize it.

Robin Sharma

When I look at people who have unusual last names, I often wonder about where they might be from and how long ago their family immigrated. Then I wonder about their circumstances in the country they left, and what led them to leave. Perhaps they searched for something better but found new and different challenges, including language barriers.

Robin's family immigrated from India to Canada in search of a better life. Robin grew up in a small town, Port Hawkesbury, Nova Scotia, Canada, and wanted to be an attorney. He pictured himself arguing important cases before a jury and fighting for justice.

His parents encouraged him to follow his dreams. He received his law degree and went to work for the Nova Scotia Supreme Court and later for the government of Canada, as a staff litigation attorney.

Even though he achieved his dream, he felt empty. He knew there had to be more to life than grinding through the legal briefs and depositions each day. He wanted to write. He felt it as a calling. He wanted his writing to inspire others to have their best life, which he also believed he would find for himself, by writing.

His mother edited his first book, *Megaliving: 30 Days to a Perfect Life.* Robin self-published it through a local Kinkos. He copied, printed, and bound a hundred copies of his book.

The book sold thirty copies, twenty-eight of which were bought by his own family. Robin did not give up.

Two years later he wrote his second book and self-published it as well, *The Monk Who Sold His Ferrari.* While this book was initially self-published, Harper Collins picked it up. It is now an international best-seller, having sold millions of copies in many different languages.

His mission with this book was to walk through his struggles on the pages, coming to a place of inner peace and success defined by his terms and not that of the world. He realized his success by helping others achieve success and peace in their lives.

In this pursuit, Robin has created a life that has made a difference in the world that is beyond quantification. He has gone from selling a few books out of the trunk of his car to working with national leaders and CEOs of some of the largest companies in the world.

What is interesting about Robin Sharma's story is not his greatness on the stage or the publishing and corporate worlds. It's how he cares for the people around him.

The other day I listened to one of his coaching sessions. Yes, I subscribe to his coaching program. I was struck by him sharing that in the middle of his busy day, he turned his car around, got out, and helped a homeless man get to a safe place. He gave him warm clothes and enough money to buy something to eat.

You don't see many people in the corporate power circuit doing that. but Robin is different. He then encouraged each of us, to open our eyes to the challenges of the people around us. We could spend a few minutes and a couple of dollars to make a difference in someone's life.

I mentioned in a previous chapter that he routinely buys a bottle of wine at a restaurant. He only takes one big glass of it and then gives the remaining portion of the bottle, to the kitchen staff for their wonderful work.

This has inspired others to do the same. He has also inspired some of those he has helped, to change their lives and begin to pursue their dreams. I learned from Robin that when you take the time to care for those around you, you are making the world a better place, one kind act at a time.

~

Do you remember the first time you watched the movie, *It's a Wonderful Life*? George Bailey was ready to give up on life, thinking he was worth more dead than alive. He wishes he'd never been born. Thankfully, Clarence grants that wish, and George gets the rare opportunity to see the world without him. Take some time to think about your life's impact on others. One good act you've done has set off immeasurable ripples into the world. Your life matters.

The difference George Bailey made by just being a good guy and helping where he could, impacted the world around him and everyone in it.

He wasn't a saint, or Mother Teresa, or Nelson Mandela. He was an ordinary guy, like you and me, doing his very best each day. That made all the difference in his life, and it does in your life and your world.

Remember the conversation with the person who thought they made no difference until we added the number of people he interacted with each day and multiplied it out? Have you calculated the number of people you interact with daily?

Twenty?

Thirty?

Add in the people who are impacted by what you say or do. With all that, you probably have a pretty big number.

If you add in the people you have smiled at or waved to, even if you only did that a few times a day, you'd brighten the day for over a hundred people over the past month.

Multiplying those numbers over a few years, you could fill Madison Square Garden to standing room only with your fans. Your smile, kind words all add up to making more of a difference than you can envision.

You matter.

If you're concerned that you aren't making a big enough positive impact on the world around you, that's okay. It's probably a healthy way to look at it. I recommend doing one thing each week for someone, in an intentional way, to help them. Commit to it. It could be someone different each week. It could be a cause or a person you find on the street. It could be a neighbor. It doesn't matter who you help, only that it is for someone who can't pay you back.

Make a plan and be intentional about it. Remember it isn't about making the biggest impact or drawing attention. It works best when no one knows that it is you, Make it anonymous.

When you do that, several things will happen.

It will have a positive influence on the life or the cause that you help.

That will initiate a ripple effect to the people encountered by those you help.

It will increase your sense of well-being and happiness more than you can imagine. Remember the positive psychology we talked about earlier.

Every day, I ask myself "who can I impact for good today or this week?" Sometimes I do not have an answer, but you would be surprised at how these opportunities present themselves when you are looking for them. God often has someone in mind.

Before you know it, you've made more worthwhile contributions to the world than you ever considered.

It's rarely the big gift that changes the world. It's the small gift, given over time, to whomever or wherever you decide, that makes the grandest change.

It forever changes the world.

Dr. Cliff Robertson, Jr.

Chapter 14

Let's Change Our World

I think we need to create an intentional plan. Where do we start?

The best place to begin is right where you are. Mother Teresa said, "If you want to bring happiness to the world, begin by going home and loving your family."

Maybe you love to bake, keep your home repairs done, take care of the yard, do the laundry or decorate your home out of love for your family. Doing small things, with great love, by beginning at home may be exactly what you are called to do. In doing these acts of love, you are changing the world.

Jesus said, "Love thy neighbor, as thyself."

If we are to do that, that means we must begin with loving ourselves. This could mean taking time to put down our phones and reading a good book. Going for a walk or even taking an afternoon nap. Maybe we need to see a counselor to help us work through some challenges we are facing. Love yourself enough to say no to the world for a moment, so you can say yes to yourself. Self-care is essential. After all, how are we to be able to love another, if we do not first love ourselves?

Now, let's talk about that neighbor. Maybe you just reach out to your next-door neighbor and do something nice for them. When was the last time you spoke to your neighbor? Heck, do we even know their name?

Maybe you just don't feel comfortable with that, and you want to do something else.

Are you involved with a church? They are almost always in need of volunteers. What about local charities? They are everywhere and there is always a need there. Are you passionate about helping the homeless, the hungry, youth, women—battered, single moms, sex-trafficking victims, and more—elderly, inmates, or animals?

Some people say, "Well I give to charities, isn't that enough?"

I say that giving is important, but it isn't enough. You need to get involved. You will see things that writing a check will never show you. It will bring you joy that a few dollars can never buy. And it will enrich your life in priceless ways.

As you move forward with an intentional plan to make an even greater difference, your life will become filled with joy and happiness. If during this process, you did the multiplication exercise that I discussed earlier, I think you might find the number to be staggering.

And yet, I know that some of us are still not on board. You might think you've made so many mistakes in life, how can any of that be good?

I will answer by reminding you that you are not defined by your very worst. You are defined by who you are today and what you are striving for.

God tells us in His word that He works all things together for the good, for those that love Him and are called according to His purpose (Romans 8:28). That means that when we give our hearts and lives over to God, He takes the very best and the very worst in our lives and brings things that are even better from it.

I'm a student of the Bible with a doctorate in theology. I love to look at the origins of certain words. Take the word "good" for example. In today's context, it's thrown around and can have little to no meaning.

But when we look at "good" in the biblical context, we see it first used in the book of Genesis. In the rules of biblical translation and interpretation, the Law of First Usage reminds us of the origin and true meaning of the word. "Good" is first used to describe God's creation.

Putting all that into the context of this verse, God tells us He will take our best and make it amazing. He can even take our very worst and bring something that is creation level good from it. That gives me tremendous hope when I fail, and I fail daily. With that, I know God can pick up the pieces and make a masterpiece from them.

I've shared many stories in this book and I hope they have been inspiring to you. I want you to keep this book with you because I feel like it will help you when tough times come.

I'm not going to sugarcoat what is to come.

Life can be hard.

Tragedy can and will come our way.

203

But it's worth it.

Life is worth the struggle.

Your life is special, filled with purpose

and a divine mission that only you can fulfill.

#YourLifeMatters.

The tough times only prepare us for the better to come. There are lessons inside of the difficulties that we cannot learn any other way. These lessons—if we will let them speak to us and teach us—will change our world for the better, and make a huge difference in the world.

I promise.

What I want you to do today:

Even if you are not a person of faith, I want you to pray, "God, what can I do today to change the world?"

Then I want you to set out with the intention of keeping your mind and heart open for the opportunity that will present itself... and trust me it will. When it happens, I want you to pray, "God, thank you."

Then I want you to repeat the same thing tomorrow.

Next, I want you to do the math that we have talked about earlier. Calculate how many people you interact with, in a meaningful way, each day. Work, school, social, church, volunteer, shopping, etc. Then multiply it for a week, then a month, and over a year.

Take that yearly number and multiply it by the number of years you have lived since you started school, until now. Some of you will have been able to fill auditoriums with fans, while others will fill arenas, and still others large stadiums.

The truth is the impact that you have had on this world cannot be truly calculated. One person, who impacts one other person, creates a ripple effect that goes beyond just the two of you.

Imagine for a moment, that your help, kind act, or positive word was repeated, like an echo through a canyon. Then it was boosted by you doing it again. Then the people it touched, turned and did the same thing.

With each of us impacting one more person in a continuing ripple effect, together, we can change the world. If you doubt it, reread some of the stories.

Your story is no different.

Today, I want you to launch out with a new mindset.

"I am a world changer for good."

#MyLifeMatters.

Keep seeking God and His guidance daily and He will open doors for you that you cannot imagine even exist.

Dr. Cliff Robertson, Jr.

Epilogue

When I first started this process, I began to think about life and its beginnings and it dawned on me that life matters because it's a miracle. Every life comes to be through a process that is a miracle. The human body is a miracle-performing machine that is in no way accidental—it is purposeful and wonderful. Life is a miracle and miracles matter, so therefore your life matters, even on the most basic level. God calls you His Masterpiece.

So, no matter what you are going through today,

no matter how hard it may be,

no matter how often you want to quit or give up,

no matter the diagnosis or the disaster,

YOUR LIFE MATTERS.

~

Don't quit. Every day is a gift.

Don't give up on life—even when it seems impossible. As long as there is a breath of air in you and a beating heart, there is hope.

Maya Angelou once said, "You may encounter many defeats, but you must not be defeated. In fact, it may be necessary to encounter the defeats, so you can know who you are, what you can rise from, how you can still come out of it."

207

When we do not quit, we inspire others to say "Because of you, I didn't give up!"

Never forget

#YourLifeMatters,

no matter what.

Bibliography

Aknin, Lara B., Norton, Dunn. *The Journal of Positive Psychology*. "From wealth to well-being? Money matters, but less than people think" 2009. 4: 6, 523 — 527 http://dx.doi.org/10.1080/17439760903271421

Barraza, Jorge A, Paul Zak. "Empathy toward strangers triggers oxytocin release and subsequent generosity." https://pubmed.ncbi.nlm.nih.gov/19580564/

Biography Mother Teresa. Biography Online. https://www.biographyonline.net/nobelprize/mother_teresa.html

Butcher, Andy. "Sarah Young: Amid Suffering, Devotion Publishers Weekly, November 14, 2012 www.publishersweekly.com/pw/by-topic/industry-news/religion/article/54756-sarah-young-amid-suffering-devotion.html

Dillard et al."The Dark Side of Optimism: Unrealistic Optimism About Problems With Alcohol Predicts Subsequent Negative Event Experiences." Personality and Social Psychology Bulletin, 2009; 35 (11): 1540 DOI: 10.1177/0146167209343124

Disability in the Arab Countries: Time to Promote Identity .... https://www.ruhglobal.com/disability-in-the-arab-countries-time-to-promote-identity-awareness/

Does Advertising Affect Self-Image - 1116 Words. Bartleby. https://www.bartleby.com/essay/Does-Advertising-Affect-Self-Image-F3YF3JKS8CKDQ

Dunn, Elizabeth W., Aknin, Norton. "Spending money on others promotes happiness." https://pubmed.ncbi.nlm.nih.gov/18356530/

Dunn, Warrick. *Running for My Life*. It Books. 2009.

Effects of advertising on self-esteem – Daily Sundial. https://sundial.csun.edu/11348/archive/effectsofadvertising onselfesteem/

happiness in a large social network: longitudinal analysis over 20 years in the Framingham Heart Study." pubmed.ncbi.nlm.nih.gov/19056788/

George Muller Evangelist, Orphanages, Bristol, England https://www.wholesomewords.org/biography/bmuller2.html

Gilsdorf, JR. *Into Darkness and Silence: What Caused Helen Keller's Deafblindness?* Clin Infect Dis. 2018 Oct 15;67(9):1445-1449. doi: 10.1093/cid/ciy385. PMID: 29741601.

Gwyther, Matthew. "Editor's Letter: Dealing with Uncertainty." Management Today. Haymarket Business Publications Ltd. Dec. 2016. p. 9.

Horowitz, Tony. "Did Civil War Solidiers Have PTSD?" Smithsonian Magazine, January 2015 www.smithsonianmag.com/history/ptsd-civil-wars-hidden-legacy

How the Words of a Faithful Preacher Led Billy Graham to .... https://www.crosswalk.com/church/pastors-or-leadership/how-the-words-of-a-faithful-preacher-led-billy-graham-to-christ.html

Hopson, Jericha. *Disability as Culture*. Multicultural Education, vol. 27, no. 1. Caddo Gap Press. Oct. 2019. p. 22.

Howell, R. T., & Hill, G. "The mediators of experiential purchases: Determining the impact of psychological needs satisfaction and social comparison." *The Journal of Positive Psychology*, 4(6), 511–522. 2009. https://doi.org/10.1080/17439760903270993

Jenkinson, Caroline E, Dickens, Jones, Thompson-Coon, Taylor, Rogers, Bambra, Lang, Richards. "Is volunteering a public health intervention? A systematic review and meta-analysis of the health and survival of volunteers." https://pubmed.ncbi.nlm.nih.gov/23968220/

Kjerulf, Alexander. "Happiness at work" https://www.thenationalnews.com/business/well-being-results-and-relationships-are-the-keys-to-happiness-at-work-1.202830

Layous, Kristin, Nelson, Oberle, Schonert-Reichl, Lyumborsky. Frank Kreuger, Editor. "Kindness Counts: Prompting Prosocial Behavior in Preadolescents Boosts Peer Acceptance and Well-Being." https://www.ncbi.nlm.nih.gov/pmc/articles/PMC3530573/

Lyubomirsky, Sonja, King, Diener. "The benefits of frequent positive affect: does happiness lead to success?" https://pubmed.ncbi.nlm.nih.gov/16351326/

Orphans' Lonely Beginnings Reveal How Parents Shape A .... https://www.psychologicalscience.org/news/orphans-lonely- beginnings-reveal-how-parents-shape-a-childs-brain.html

Palau, Louis, Dr. *Where is God When Bad Things Happen.* Doubleday.   1999.

Positive Psychology Academy. https://www.nmrhca.org/wp-content/uploads/2021/12/RHCA-Positive-Psych-Academy.pdf

Positive Self-Image: How to Improve Self- and Body-Image. https://my.clevelandclinic.org/health/articles/12942-fostering-a-positive-self-image

Palihapitiya, Chamath. "Social Media is changing society." https://www.businessinsider.com/former-facebook-exec-chamath-palihapitiya-social-media-damaging-society-2017-12

Self-image: The guide on how to create a grand self-image. https://www.grandself.com/self-image/

Scott, B. A., & Barnes, C. M. (2011). "A multilevel field investigation of emotional labor, affect work withdrawal, and gender." *Academy of Management Journal*, 54(1), 116–136. https://psycnet.apa.org/record/2011-07261-006

Seligman, M. E. P., Steen, T. A., Park, N., & Peterson, C. (2005). "Positive Psychology Progress: Empirical Validation of Interventions." *American Psychologist*, 60(5), 410–421. 2005.https://doi.org/10.1037/0003-066X.60.5.410

Social Media Affects Our Brains: Learn How to Immediately .... https://lagosmums.com/social-media-affects-our-brains/

The Ripple Effect of Suicide | NAMI: National Alliance on https://nami.org/Blogs/NAMI-Blog/September-2018/The-Ripple-Effect-of-Suicide

This is Your Brain on Instagram: Effects of Social Media .... https://now.northropgrumman.com/this-is-your-brain-on-instagram-effects-of-social-media-on-the-brain/

Understanding the Neural Basis of Fear to Transform our .... https://adaa.org/learn-from-us/from-the-experts/blog-posts/professional/understanding-neural-basis-fear-transform

What is the cultural model of disability?. https://philosophy-question.com/library/lecture/read/361519-what-is-the-cultural-model-of-disability

What Is Life Purpose? | Taking Charge of Your Health ....
https://www.takingcharge.csh.umn.edu/what-life-purpose

Wilkerson, David. *The Cross and the Switchblade.* Reprint edition. Berkley. 1986

Wilkinson, Bruce. *The Prayer of Jabez*. Multnomah. 2000

Zouareg, Nordine. "Mental Health and Social Media" *Mental Health Foundation.* https://mentalhealthfoundation.org/mental-health-and-social-media/

Dr. Cliff Robertson, Jr.

Additional Resources

ErinandBen.co

JoyceMeyer.org

National Suicide Prevention Lifeline
    Hours: Available 24 hours.
    Languages: English, Spanish.
    800-273-8255
    suicidepreventionlifeline.org

National Institute of Health and National Institute of Mental
    Health https://www.nimh.nih.gov/

RobinSharma.com

TonyRobbins.com

About the Author

Cliff Robertson, Jr. M.Div, ThD. is a devoted husband to his lovely bride, Karen. He has two sons, of whom he is very proud. Dr. Robertson holds degrees in Biblical Studies, Divinity, Theology, Psychology, and Counseling. He founded The Warriors Refuge – veteran's homeless shelter, counseling center, and vocational training facility.

- Follow his author page on Amazon.com for all his books.
- Follow his blog for events, updates, and encouragement. https://drcliffrobertsonjr.com/
- Email him for speaking/preaching opportunities at drcliff@thewarriorsrefuge.us.

Other books by Dr. Robertson

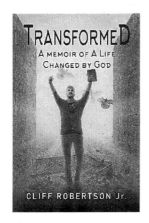

Transformed

A Memoir of a Life Changed by God

The memoir of one man who had financial success, but his life choices cost him his family, his job, his possessions, and his freedom. Behind prison bars, he realized the enormity of how his past choices impacted his family and himself. No longer willing to continue making the same crucial mistakes, he surrendered his life to God and began a complete transformation.

Made in the USA
Columbia, SC
22 March 2022

57938311R00131